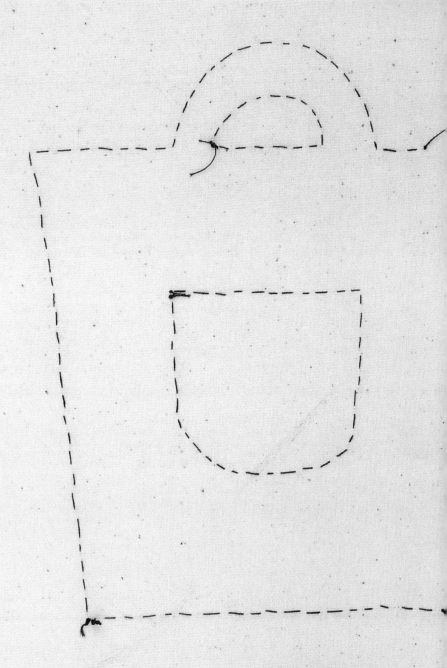

Free-Style Handmade Bags & Skirts
Copyright © Woongjin Think Big Co., LTD
English language rights, translation & production by
World Book Media LLC. For international rights inquiries contact:
info@worldbookmedia.com
First published in the United States of America by
North Light Books, an imprint of F+W Publications, Inc.,
4700 East Galbraith Road, Cincinnati, Ohio 45236. (800) 289-0963.
First edition 2008

Distributed in Canada by Fraser Direct
100 Armstrong Avenue
Georgetown, ON, Canada L7G 5S4
Tel: (905) 877-4411

Distributed in the U.K. and Europe by David & Charles
Brunel House, Newton Abbot, Devon, TQ12 4PU, England
Tel: (+44) 1626 323200, Fax: (+44) 1626 323319
E-mail: postmaster@davidandcharles.co.uk

Distributed in Australia by Capricorn Link
P.O. Box 704, S. Windsor, NSW 2756 Australia
Tel: (02) 4577-3555

Library of Congress Cataloging-in-Publication Data
Editors at Woongjin Publishing
Free-Style Handmade Bags & Skirts / Editors at Woongjin Publishing
p.   cm.
ISBN: 1-60061-196-6
ISBN: 978-1-60061-196-4

12   11   10   09   08   5   4   3   2   1

Printed in China

F+W PUBLICATIONS, INC.
www.fwpublications.com

Free-Style Handmade Bags & Skirts

Editors of Woongjin Publishing

NORTH LIGHT BOOKS

Cincinnati, Ohio
www.mycraftivity.com

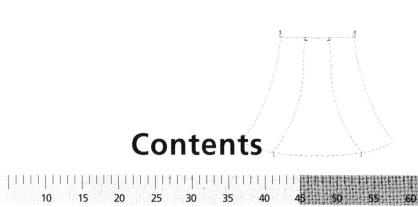

Contents

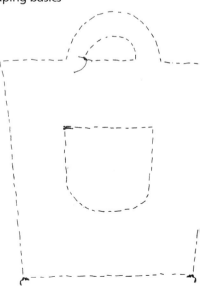

How to use this book

› UNDERSTANDING THE INSTRUCTIONS

Each project includes complete cutting, sewing, and finishing instructions that work hand-in-hand with the technical illustrations. All measurements are given in the imperial system. Techniques that have been taught elsewhere are cross-referenced as they appear again.

› READING THE ILLUSTRATIONS

Each illustration shows cutting and sewing instructions. Some sketches show placement of patterns on fabric and other preparations may not correspond to specific project steps. Step sketches are numbered per the numbers in the sewing instructions. One illustration may show several sewing steps in series.

› USING THE PATTERNS

This book includes patterns for seventeen of the bag and skirt projects, which are printed on folded sheets at the back of the book. (The other projects feature pattern pieces that are easily drafted without patterns.) Skirt patterns are based on a standard size 4 (25"–26" [64–66 cm] waist); pattern sizes can be adjusted by referring to the measurement table and alteration methods on pages 12–13. Two to three patterns are on one side of the pattern paper, overlapping, each in a different color. To preserve the original pattern, trace or copy the patterns onto separate pieces of paper.

› SELECTING FABRICS

Most fabrics are available in widths of 36", 45", and 60" (90 cm, 115 cm, and 150 cm). The width of the fabric in a project will help determine the ideal placement of a project's pattern piece, but fabrics with different widths can always be used. If a fabric has a width other than the one recommended, try to reorient the patterns so that less fabric is cut away and wasted. Patterns are usually placed along the grainline of fabric.

› MODIFYING DESIGNS

Some of these projects are made with lightweight fabric ideal for summer and spring, but the designs themselves are suitable for all seasons. By varying and experimenting with fabric weight, color, and design, a year's worth of hand-crafted pieces can be created. Also, experimenting with thread, contrasting fabrics, and trims will result in pieces that suit anyone's taste.

› SEWING MACHINE THREAD AND NEEDLES

Fine- to medium-weight cotton thread and a size 11 sewing machine needle can be used for all projects. The size of the needle should be adjusted according to the weight of each fabric; for example, use a size 9 for lighter-weight fabrics and size 14 for heavyweight fabrics. Sewing with heavyweight fabrics such as denim may require heavier-weight sewing supplies.

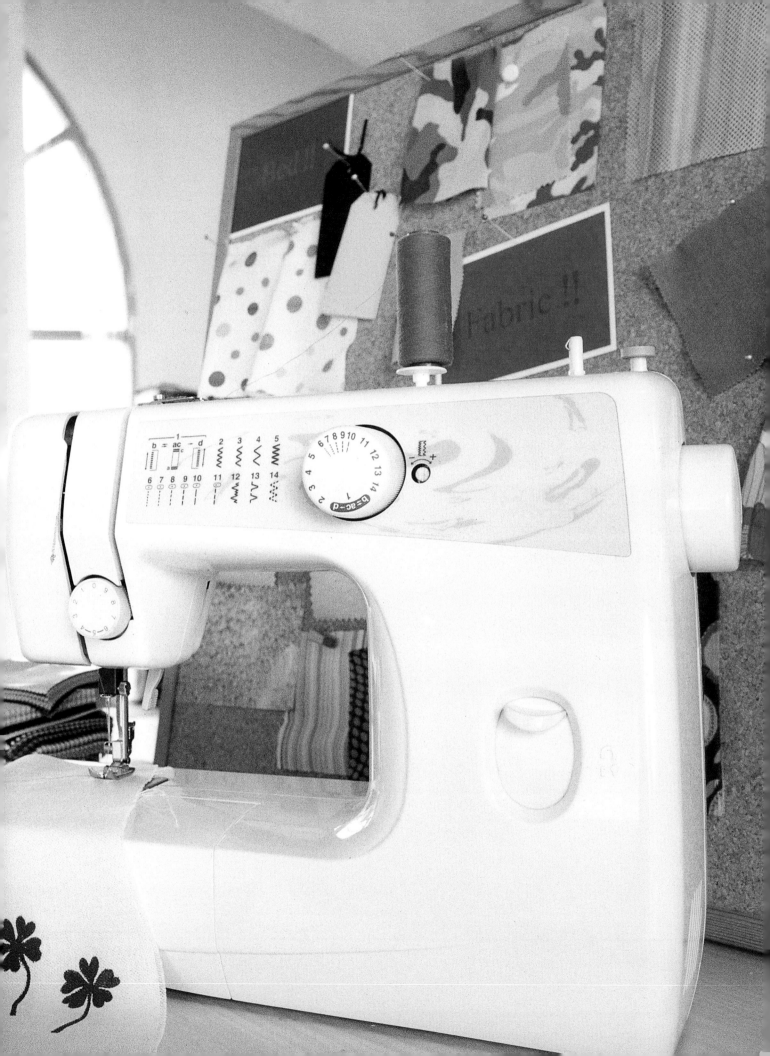

Introduction

Fashionable clothes and accessories created by hand? Even if you are inspired by DIY projects, the very idea of taking scissors, needles, and thread to fabric may still feel daunting. If you do not have a sewing machine, you may feel as though you cannot even get started. Moreover, there are so many fashions available in infinite styles these days, the process of hunting for fabric and sewing for hours to make a single item may sound excessive. What is needed instead is a fresh, modern perspective on sewing!

Sewing machines have a different meaning now than they had for our mothers and grandmothers, when they were essential tools for making clothing and accessories. Though they are no longer standard equipment for every home, they can still play an essential role in cultivating personal style. The effort you put into picking out the perfect item that suits your particular taste among thousands of designs is not to be minimized. Also, the DIY ethos of "re-make" and garment reconstruction is a design (and almost lifestyle) philosophy, not just a method for recycling used clothes. If you infuse each piece with your own ideas and creative energy, you can design and create pieces that are completely your own.

Being comfortable with a sewing machine is an essential part of sewing, but this skill is more accessible than ever before. There are many reasonably priced home sewing machines available that are easy to use. Sewing machines with basic functions such as straight stitch, zigzag stitch, and buttonhole stitch are suitable for most projects in this book.

Free-Style Handmade Bags and Skirts is packed with hardworking and inspiring content for passionate crafters who are new to sewing and eager to make unique projects. These fifty clever skirts and bags were designed by fashionistas, trendsetters, and everyday crafters. You are sure to find something new and exciting in every chapter. Each piece captures the freewheeling fashion sense of each designer's style. Sewing and experimenting with these projects will help you hone your very own personal style, too!

Sewing and Pattern-Making Basics

Milky White Handbag

Beaded Denim Skirt

Appliqué Bag with
Wooden Handle

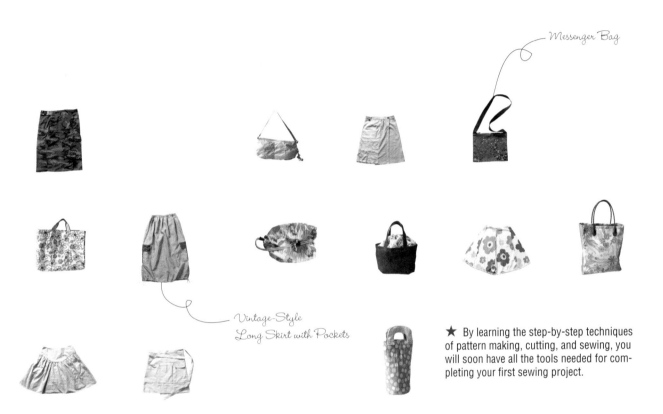

Messenger Bag

*Vintage-Style
Long Skirt with Pockets*

★ By learning the step-by-step techniques of pattern making, cutting, and sewing, you will soon have all the tools needed for completing your first sewing project.

01 pattern : creating and using sewing patterns

★ About the Patterns

First, let's get familiar with the basic measurements of your figure and how to read pattern markings.

❭ MEASUREMENTS

All skirt patterns are based on a standard size 4, but since size 4 may vary from brand to brand, the typical measurements of the size is noted. Since hip-hugging styles are included in this book's designs, the actual waist measurement of each finished skirt varies from project to project. The sample pattern can always be hemmed or adjusted to your height and taste.

Size Chart

	4 (25-26")	8 (27-28")	10-12 (29-30")
Waist	24¾" (26"[66 cm])	26¾" (28"[71 cm])	28¼" (30"[76 cm])
Hip	35⅜" (36½"[93 cm])	37⅜" (38½"[98 cm])	39¼" (41"[104 cm])

❭ UNDERSTANDING PATTERN MARKINGS

Each pattern piece includes symbols as shown in the illustration at right.

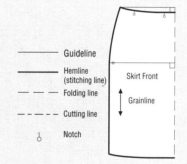

- —————— Guideline
- —————— Hemline (stitching line)
- — — — — Folding line
- – ·· – ·· – Cutting line
- ⌐⌐ Notch

Skirt Front
Grainline

NOTCHES

Bag Bottom

Bag Side

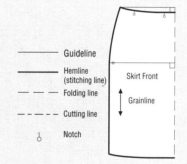

Fabric
Pattern

when pinning the pattern and fabric together, make a ¼" (0.5 cm) clip at the seam allowance

Notches are used to align pieces sewn together. Copy these notches onto the cut fabric pieces. Transfer these symbols with a chalk pen or chalk paper (which brushes off easily). Also, you can make small snips (¼" [0.5 cm] long) with scissors in the seam allowance to mark the notches.

★ Pattern-Making Process

1 Detach the folded patterns enclosed at the end of the book.

2 Trace the pattern.

Because multiple pattern pieces share a page, the traced pattern outlines will be easier to follow in Step 3. Use a different color pen for a project's multiple pattern pieces, such as a skirt front and back.)

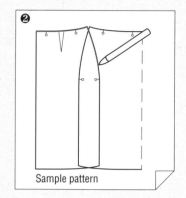

Sample pattern

3 Copy the pattern to a separate piece of paper.

To preserve the original pattern pages, copy the pattern onto a separate piece of paper. Lay a piece of tracing paper or vellum on top of the pattern and trace the pattern. Be sure to mark the darts and notches as well. Write the names of each pattern piece on the traced pattern so they are easily identified.

Paper for copying the pattern

4 Cut out the pattern.

The enclosed patterns do not have seam allowances. Cut the pattern pieces along the seamline. When cutting the fabric, add about ¼" (0.6 cm) to all sides for the seam allowance. Alternatively, seam allowances can be added when transferring the pattern to tracing paper or vellum.

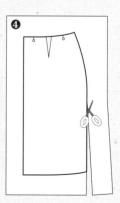

★ Altering Patterns to Fit Your Figure

When you want to change the silhouette of a design, adjust the size, or alter the fit for lighter- or heavier-weight fabrics, adjust the pattern lines and measurements as shown in the illustrations below.

1 Draw guidelines.

Draw alteration guidelines that are perpendicular to the center front and center back of the skirt pattern, as shown at right.

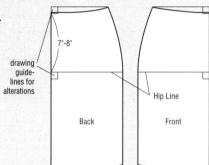

drawing guidelines for alterations

7"-8"

Hip Line

Back   Front

2 Adjust the waistline.

To increase the waist measurement, add one quarter of the total waist measurement increase to each side seam. To reduce the waist measurement, subtract one quarter of the total waist measurement reduction from each side seam.

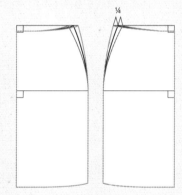

¼

3 Adjust the hip.

Alter the hip measurement by adding or subtracting one quarter of the total measurement adjustment from each side seam.

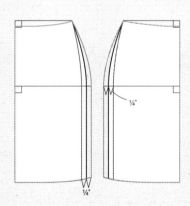

¼"

¼"

4 Adjust the length of a skirt.

For slight adjustments to a gathered or a tight skirt, simply move the hemline straight up or down (below, left). When lengthening a tight skirt by a large amount, the length of the slit should be adjusted as well. When lengthening an A-line or a flare skirt, the curve of the side seam should be adjusted to maintain the silhouette of the skirt (below, center and right).

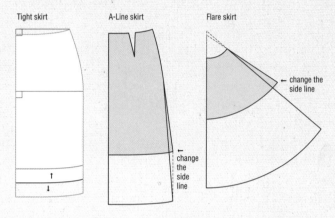

Tight skirt   A-Line skirt   Flare skirt

← change the side line

← change the side line

WHAT HIP MEASUREMENT FITS YOUR FIGURE?

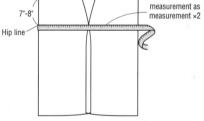

7"-8"

Hip line

measurement as measurement ×2

When the pattern pieces are lined up side by side as shown, measure the hip width and multiply it by two. If the measurement is 1½"–2⅜" (4–6 cm) larger than your actual hip measurement, the pattern is suitable for your size. If the difference is larger or smaller, alter the pattern as needed by following the pattern alteration techniques on this page.

02 tools : basic sewing tools

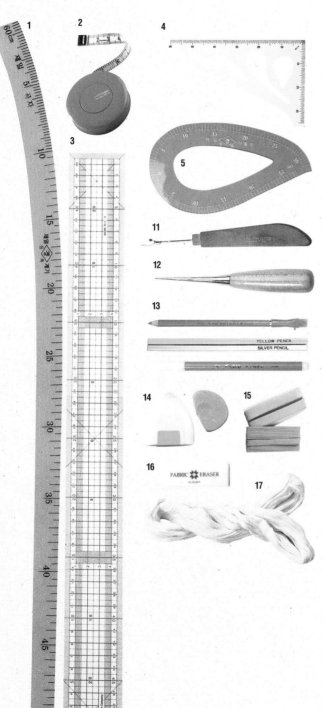

★ Basic Cutting and Sewing Tools

1 Curved ruler Used for drawing smooth, curved lines, such as a skirt's seamline. **2 Tape measure** Used for taking body measurements. **3 Clear graph (or quilter's) ruler** Available in a wide range of sizes and dimensions; the graph is helpful for drawing even seam allowances. **4 L-Square** Used for drawing 90-degree angles. **5 French curve** Used for drawing smaller, detailed curves, such as decorative components or appliqué. **6 Serrated-edge scissors** The serrated edges create a clean cut in the fabric without the fabric slipping between the blades. **7 Bent-handled tailor's scissors** Scissors specially designed for the smooth cutting of long lengths of fabric. **8 Thread clippers** Sharp clippers used for snipping thread, including cutting thread after sewing or neatening thread tails. **9 Needles and thread** The needles used in home sewing machines are available in sizes 9, 11, 14, and 16. The higher the size number, the thicker the needle is. Size 9 is suitable for lightweight fabrics, such as silk; medium-weight fabrics such as oxford can be sewn with size 11. Sizes 14 to 16 needles are suitable for terrycloth, denim, or corduroy fabrics. The number of a hand-sewing needle size decreases as the shaft gets thicker. Threads are available in cotton, silk, polyester, and other fiber blends. Thread should be chosen based on the fabric's fiber content and its color. **10 Pins and pincushion** Pins hold fabric and patterns in place before and during sewing. **11 Seam ripper** Its extremely sharp hook is used for opening seams. **12 Awl or stiletto** Its sharp tip makes holes in leather or thick fabrics or shapes sewn corners. **13 Chalk marking tools** Specially designed implements are used to draw lines on fabric without leaving any residue on your fingers. Also available are water-soluble chalk pens, whose marks can be removed with water and are easy to correct. **14 Chalk** Most sewing chalk is available in triangular wedges for easy handling. Some are available with a plastic cover to keep the hands dust-free. **15 Bias tape** Used to bind edges, such as seams and bag openings. It is available in various colors, prints, and sizes. **16 Fabric eraser** Used for removing unwanted chalk marks on fabrics. **17 Basting thread** Used for basting by hand with a hand-sewing needle. To use, cut the end of the bundle and pull out one thread at a time.

★ Clever Sewing Tools

1 Heat-sensitive chalk pens The ink is water soluble and the marks disappear when the fabric is ironed. **2 Mechanical pencils for fabrics** The yellow chalk lead makes lines easily visible when marking dark fabrics. The thin lead draws very detailed lines. The chalk marks should always be removed (or erased) before ironing the fabric, otherwise they will be permanently heat-set. **3 Fabric glue pen** Fabric glue secures difficult folds or hems. Make fold lines with your fingertips on seam allowances or piping areas. Add water to the pen and put 5-6 drops of the substance where needed. Glue is especially helpful when the direction of the bias or overlapping fabric inhibits easy sewing. **4 Seam folder** Used for opening or folding seams or for folding fabrics in general. Lines can be marked on fabrics using the opposite (handle) end of the tool. **5 Rotary cutter** This tool has an extremely sharp, circular, 45-mm-diameter blade that enables smooth cutting of long, curved lines and multiple layers of fabric. When using a rotary cutter, always protect the work surface with a self-healing cutting mat. **6 Pin magnet** The magnet within keeps pins in place and accessible. **7 Mini-iron** Useful for seam finishing as well as patchwork and appliqué. **8 Chalk paper** Double-faced carbon paper designed for marking on fabrics. Place it between two pieces of fabric and trace or duplicate patterns with a tracing wheel. The carbon marks are water soluble. **9 Tracing wheel (or roulette)** Used for copying cutting lines and notches in patterns with chalk paper. **10 Rivets and rivet-setting tool** This rod-shaped tool, plus a hammer or mallet, is used for setting rivets in fabric. **11 Bias tape maker** To create coordinating bias tape, feed narrow strips of fabric through this tool. **12 Eyelet pliers** These pliers are used to set eyelets in fabric. To set an eyelet: Place a protective mat beneath the fabric and use a punch to make a hole. Insert the eyelet into the pliers and press it to set the eyelet into the hole. **13 Multipurpose work surface** With three different faces—each made of a different material (sandpaper, rubber, and ironing board)—this tool aids in pattern drawing, cutting, and ironing.

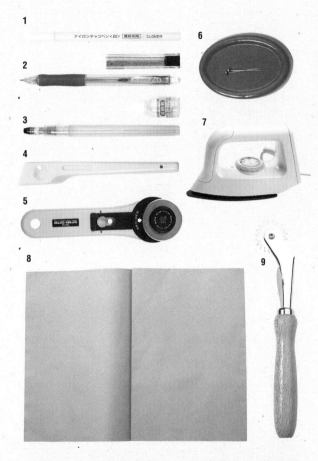

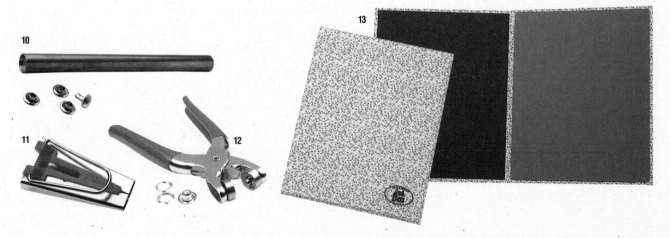

03 cutting : cutting fabrics

★ Selecting Fabric

Fabrics vary in structure (or weave), fiber content, and weight. Most cotton fabrics are appropriate for skirt making; in particular, gingham and khaki are easy to handle and are appropriate for warm weather. Corduroy and denim are sturdy and practical choices for skirts but are slightly more challenging to sew. For light, romantic styles, select fabrics such as silk and satin. Wool fabrics, such as gabardine (a sturdy, durable wool), flannel (a soft, lightweight wool), and tweed (made from thick wool yarn) are suitable for cooler weather.

Durable fabrics, such as upholstery fabric, denim, nylon, and polyester, are appropriate for bags. Since bag linings are mostly for reinforcing the main fabric or hiding the seams, they are usually made from cotton fabrics that are lighter in weight than the main fabric. Lining fabrics can either match the main fabric color for a clean look or create contrast with a printed design.

Also, fusible interfacing can be applied to the wrong side of the fabric for structured bags and for strengthening lightweight fabric bags.

STABILIZING FABRICS WITH FUSIBLE INTERFACING

Fusible interfacings have web-like structures and adhesive properties, and are used for enhancing the durability of fabrics. When fusible interfacing is applied to cut fabric, the fabric is stiffened, enabling it to hold its shape. Among fusible interfacings, iron-on styles are the easiest to use. Some fusible materials rely on peel-and-stick adhesives.

To apply fusible (heat-set) interfacing, lay the main fabric flat, right side down, and place the fusible interfacing's adhesive (shiny) side to the wrong side of main fabric. Place a piece of lightweight, scrap fabric on top of both layers to prevent the adhesive from sticking to the iron. The iron should be in dry mode and set to about 150ºF (65°C). Press.

For project pieces that require fusible interfacing, a separate pattern piece should be made for it. The fusible interfacing should measure about ⅛"–¼" (0.3 cm–0.5 cm) larger than the seamline of the fabric. Excess interfacing can be trimmed from the seam allowances after sewing.

Fabric interfacings are used to stabilize waistbands, and are made of thick cotton or silk. Use thick cotton interfacing for heavy fabrics and silk interfacing for lightweight fabrics.

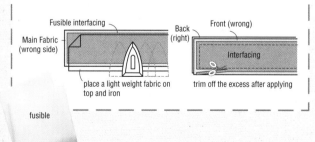

Main Fabric (wrong side) / Fusible interfacing / Back (right) / Front (wrong) / Interfacing / place a light weight fabric on top and iron / trim off the excess after applying

fusible

★ Grainline of Fabric

With only a quick look at the weave of any fabric, it may appear that both directions of the fabric are the same. But when the fabric is stretched in each direction, there is some difference in elasticity. The direction in which the fabric does not stretch is called the fabric grain, or grainline. The direction that does stretch is the horizontal direction, the cross-grain. The direction with the most elasticity lies along a 45-degree diagonal called the bias.

Since most skirts need some elasticity around the hips, properly orienting the pattern along the grain is essential. For bags, the pattern must be placed along the grain to minimize vertical stretch. Projects using synthetic fabrics with no elasticity, such as plastic, can be laid out in any direction.

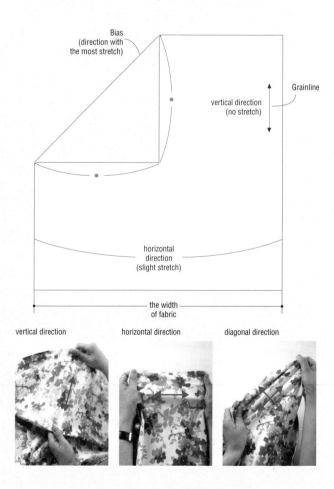

Bias (direction with the most stretch)

Grainline

vertical direction (no stretch)

horizontal direction (slight stretch)

the width of fabric

vertical direction   horizontal direction   diagonal direction

★ Pattern Placement

Fabrics vary in width—36", 45", and 60" (90 cm, 110 cm and 150 cm) — so the orientation and layout of patterns should be adjusted based on the width of the fabric. For most projects, follow the pattern placement as shown in the illustrations. If the illustration is not available, place the bigger patterns first. Smaller patterns, such as belts, handles, and pockets, can be laid out in the remaining space. Also, in order to use the fabric most efficiently, the front and back panels can be placed upside down. (However, when the fabric has a unidirectional texture or is a printed fabric with a directional pattern, this is not an option.) When using print fabric, such as plaids and stripes, always purchase more fabric than the project calls for, since pattern pieces need to be oriented precisely to align the print properly in the finished garment. When making a skirt with big floral prints, however, offsetting the flowers slightly on both side seams will create a pleasing visual balance.

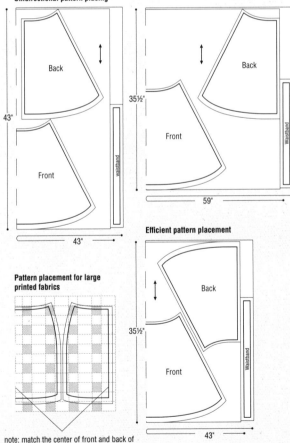

Unidirectional pattern placing

Pattern placement for large printed fabrics

note: match the center of front and back of the skirt to the center of the print pattern.

Efficient pattern placement

★ Cutting

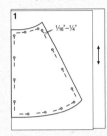 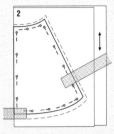 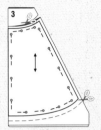

After planning the layout of the pattern pieces, pin the pattern pieces the fabric. Pin lightly inside the seamline so the chalk paper can be inserted between the layers of fabric. When pinning straight lines, leave ¼"–½" (0.6 cm–1.3 cm) between pins. For curved lines, place pins more tightly together, and pin the center of curve as well. (Figure 1)

Using a chalk wedge or pen, add seam allowances. If the seamlines have not already been marked, draw them as well. (A clear quilter's ruler is helpful for drawing seam allowances.) (Figure 2)

While the pattern is still pinned to the fabric, cut the fabric along the seam allowance using bent-handled tailor's scissors. When cutting a curved line that connects to a straight line, fold the straight line along the seamline first, and then cut. (Figure 3)

USING A TRACING WHEEL

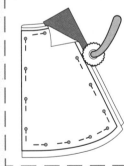

After cutting the folded fabric, wrong sides together, insert the carbon paper between the two layers and trace the seamlines using a tracing wheel. This action will draw the seamlines inside the fabric.

04 making : basic sewing techniques

★ Basic Parts of a Sewing Machine

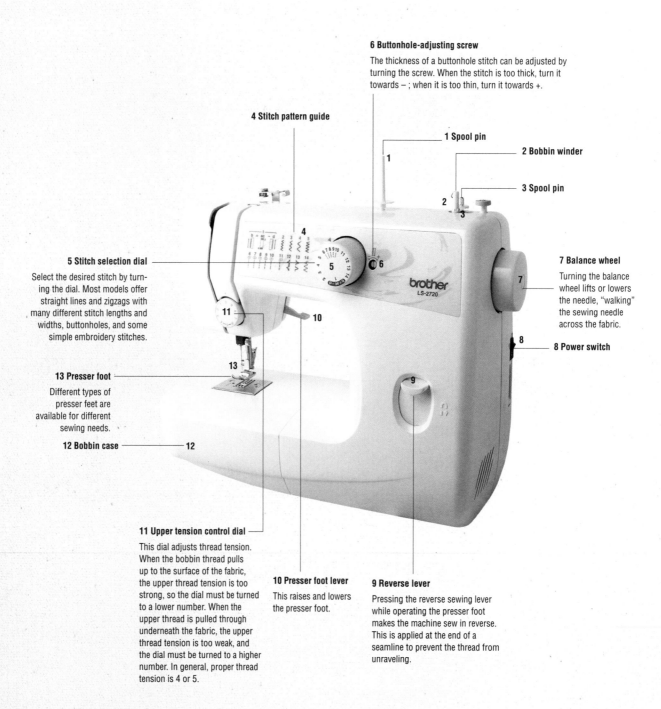

6 Buttonhole-adjusting screw
The thickness of a buttonhole stitch can be adjusted by turning the screw. When the stitch is too thick, turn it towards − ; when it is too thin, turn it towards +.

4 Stitch pattern guide

1 Spool pin

2 Bobbin winder

3 Spool pin

5 Stitch selection dial
Select the desired stitch by turning the dial. Most models offer straight lines and zigzags with many different stitch lengths and widths, buttonholes, and some simple embroidery stitches.

7 Balance wheel
Turning the balance wheel lifts or lowers the needle, "walking" the sewing needle across the fabric.

8 Power switch

13 Presser foot
Different types of presser feet are available for different sewing needs.

12 Bobbin case

11 Upper tension control dial
This dial adjusts thread tension. When the bobbin thread pulls up to the surface of the fabric, the upper thread tension is too strong, so the dial must be turned to a lower number. When the upper thread is pulled through underneath the fabric, the upper thread tension is too weak, and the dial must be turned to a higher number. In general, proper thread tension is 4 or 5.

10 Presser foot lever
This raises and lowers the presser foot.

9 Reverse lever
Pressing the reverse sewing lever while operating the presser foot makes the machine sew in reverse. This is applied at the end of a seamline to prevent the thread from unraveling.

★ Basting Stitch

A basting stitch holds together multiple fabric layers, before a seam is machine stitched. It is more secure than pins. After pinning the fabric together, the basting stitch is applied outside the seamlines. Use longer stitches for straight lines and shorter stitches for curved lines.

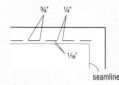

¾" ¼"

¹⁄₁₆"

seamline

TYPES OF PRESSER FEET

1   2   3   4   5

1 Zigzag foot is standard with most sewing machines. It is used to make most stitches, including zigzag stitches, buttonhole stitches, overlock stitches, blind-hemming stitches, and straight stitches. There is a special foot designed for straight-line sewing.

2 Zipper foot Also called a one-toe foot or piping foot, it has a single pressure prong for one side of the needle (most feet have prongs that flank the needle). It is ideal for inserting zippers and covering cords.

3 Rolled hem foot Allows a raw edge of fabric to be clean-finished.

4 Buttonhole foot This foot creates a buttonhole in the exact size needed.

5 Button-sewing foot This foot is used for ensuring even sewing of buttons on skirts or pants.

There are many types of feet for many purposes, such as for shirring, overlocking, blind hemming, and quilting and feet for leather and knit fabrics. For the invisible zippers used in many of this book's projects, an invisible-zipper foot can be used instead of the one-toe foot.

BALANCING THE HEIGHT OF THE NEEDLE AND PRESSER FOOT

When sewing thicker layers of fabrics, such as pleats or layered seams, feed the fabric inside the foot using an awl or needle tool. Alternatively, a thick piece of paper can be placed underneath one half of the foot to balance the height between the needle and the foot. When the height is balanced, the sewing is more stable. When sewing lightweight fabrics, a thin piece of paper, such as tracing paper, can be placed between the presser foot and the fabric, and sewn to the fabric. The paper is torn off after sewing.

fold a postcard in half, or use a thick piece of paper

★ Machine Sewing Basics

› SEWING STRAIGHT LINES

The following are basic instructions for sewing the bags and skirts in this book. Attach the presser foot and thread the machine, then:

1 Insert the needle into the fabric at the beginning of the seamline. (If beginning with reverse stitching, place the needle slightly forward of the starting point.) Set the stitch length dial to 1.5–2. Standard stitch length is 10–12 stitches per inch (about 2.5 cm).

2 Start stitching slowly and accelerate to a comfortable speed. Place your left hand behind the foot and your right hand between you and the needle, then gently pull the fabric taut. Hand placement will differ from person to person, so find the best position for you.

3 Slow down as the end of the seamline approaches. Reverse stitch to secure the thread.

4 To change sewing direction, stop sewing, then turn the balance wheel to hand-walk the needle to the turning point. With the needle still inserted in the fabric, lift up the presser foot and turn the fabric. Lower the presser foot and continue sewing along the seamline.

› SEWING CURVED LINES

Place your hand closer to the needle for added fabric control. Wrinkles in curved seams can be avoided by pinning or basting the fabric before sewing. Sew curves slowly, and pause several times during sewing to adjust the fabric. Occasionally lift the presser foot lever with your right hand and turn the fabric with your left hand.

› TOPSTITCHING SEAMS

Topstitching can be added along on the edges of a seam, as shown in the illustrations at right. These stitches are ¹⁄₁₆"–⅛" (0.1 cm–0.3 cm) away from the seamline. Topstitching creates a more secure seam and adds decoration. Since topstitching is visible, the thread color should be considered.

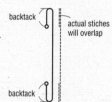

backtack   actual stiches will overlap

backtack

sewing a straight line

sewing a curved line

sewing a curved line

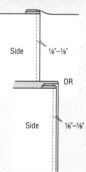

Side   ⅛"–⅛"

OR

Side   ⅛"–⅛"

★ Finishing Seams 101

If seams and hems are not finished properly, the fabric edges
will fray when the garment or accessory is laundered.
The following hem-finishing methods prevent frayed edges.

› PINKING THE EDGES

For most woven cotton fabrics, this is the easiest finishing
method. With pinking shears, cut along the fabric edges,
creating a zigzag finish.

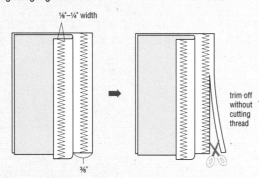

› OVERLOCK STITCHING (SERGING)

An overlocking machine (or a serger)
cuts the excess fabric from a seam as it
is sewn. Always leave a sufficient seam
allowance, about ¼" (0.5 cm).

Note: If you do not have a serger, you
can zigzag stitch along the fabric edge to
finish them and prevent raveling.

› FOLDED-SEAM FINISH

To create a stronger finished seam, fold
in ¼" (0.5 cm) from the edge and press
the seam open, leaving sufficient seam
allowance.

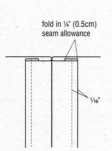

★ Hemming 101

Skirt hems are usually double-folded. Press the folded lines
for a crisp, clean look.

› FOLDING A DOUBLE-FOLDED HEM

Cut a piece of thick paper 8" (20 cm) long and 2"–2⅜" (5 cm–6 cm)
wide to create a ruler exclusively for ironing, as shown in the
drawing below. When making a double-folded hem, fold the
fabric to the ⅜" (1 cm) line and press. Finish the hem by folding
and pressing again, matching the fold to the desired width on the
ruler. Alternatively, a clear graph ruler could be used.

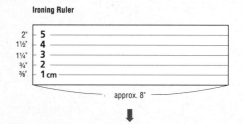

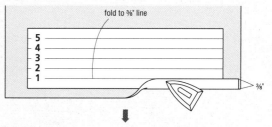

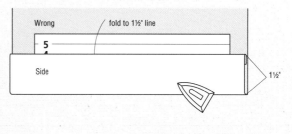

› SEWING A DOUBLE-FOLDED HEM

When a visible seamline is acceptable, sew straight across the skirt hem. After securing the fabric with pins, baste stitch or apply double-sided tape to hold the fabric together. A clean, finished hemline can be sewn just above the basting stitch. If sewing with sheer fabric, double-fold the same amount of fabric at the hem. For a ruffled, lightweight skirt, sew the folded hem as shown in the illustration, fold again, and sew on top of the previous seamline. The hem can also be hand-sewn for a soft, handmade look.

★ Finishing and Pressing

To ensure a clean finish to a garment, the seams must be pressed between sewing steps. Finished items should be lightly pressed with a thin piece of paper placed on top. When pressing seams, always apply downward pressure with the iron, instead of pressing forward.

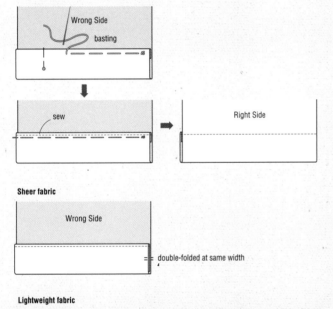

Regular fabric

Wrong Side

basting

sew

Right Side

Sheer fabric

Wrong Side

double-folded at same width

Lightweight fabric

Wrong Side

sew   ⅛"–¼"

fold again and iron

overlap to the previous stitched line

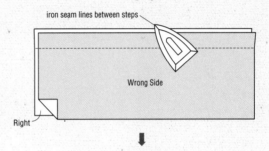

iron seam lines between steps

Wrong Side

Right

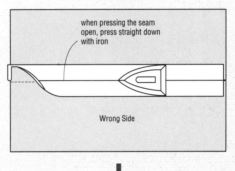

when pressing the seam open, press straight down with iron

Wrong Side

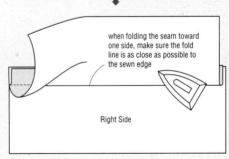

when folding the seam toward one side, make sure the fold line is as close as possible to the sewn edge

Right Side

★ Making a Basic Skirt

Before beginning one of the projects in the book, practice making a basic A-line skirt. Other projects will be much easier once you are familiar with making a basic skirt.

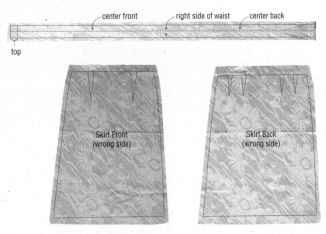

1 Refer to the previous chapter on basic tools and pattern making. After making pattern pieces for the front, back, and waistband, transfer them onto fabric and cut them, including the seam allowances. The back panel has two darts (one on each side) to account for the curve of the hip. It is recommended that the darts be marked using chalk paper or a tracing wheel. Serge the fabric edges before sewing.

2 From the wrong side, fold the darts through each dart's center. Secure the darts with pins and sew the front and back darts. The beginning and end of each dart's seamline should be backtacked (reverse stitched) for secure stitching.

3 Press each dart toward the center.

4 Sew the side seams: after placing the right sides of the front and back panels together, pin them in place and sew the side seams.

5 Press the side seams open.

6 Sew the hem: The total seam allowance for the hem is 2" (5 cm). Turn fabric up ⅜" (1 cm) and press. Turn up 1½" (4 cm) again and press. After pinning the hem, stitch along the seamline.

7 Attach the zipper on the side. (See page 120 for instructions on inserting a zipper.) When inserting an invisible zipper, place double-sided tape on both sides of the zipper tape to keep it in place. (See page 54 for instructions on inserting an invisible zipper.)

8 Place the belting (which is generally ¾"–1¼" [2 cm–3 cm] wide) on the facing side of the waistband and secure it with pins. Iron-on fusible interfacing stabilizes the waistband. Fold 1/16" (0.2 cm) from the other end and press it.

9 Place the right sides of the waistband together with the belting attached to the skirt. Line up the seamline and notches and pin or baste the seams. Sew the two pieces together. Be careful not to catch the belting when sewing.

10 Trim the excess seam allowances to minimize bulk.

11 Turn up the end of the belt with the folded edge to wrap the belting. Fold in the seam allowance of both ends of the belt, then fold the bottom seam allowance for a clean look. Pin it to hold the shape.

12 Sew the waistband facing 1/16" (0.2 cm) below the stitch line sewn in Step 9, so the stitches will be hidden. (In Step 8, be sure there is enough seam allowance to create both sides of the waistband.)

13 Press waistband and add topstitching along the waistband's edge.

14 If using snaps as a closure instead of a zipper, sew three to four snaps at the side opening after finishing the waistband. Finish the skirt by adding the hook and bar at each end of the waistband. (See page 120 for instructions on attaching a hook and bar.)

15 Press the skirt for the finishing touch.

★ Making a Basic Bag

A basic shoulder bag is a good starter project. A layer of heat-set fusible interfacing stabilizes the bag. Ready-made handles upgrade the style.

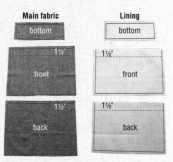

1 Cut two pieces each for the bag body (front and back), lining, and bottom. Purchase ready-made leather handles for the bag. Leave a ⅜" (1 cm) seam allowance around all edges of the pieces except the opening edge of the lining. Overlock all fabric edges before sewing. Press the iron-on fusible interfacing onto the fabric, aligning it with the seamline. In general, only the bag body needs fusible interfacing, but if the lining fabric is thin or lightweight, the fusible interfacing can be fixed to the lining as well.

2 Sew each component of the bag body (front and back): With right sides together, sew both side seams. Backtack (reverse stitch) at the beginning and end of each side seam. Press the seam open.

3 Align the bottom with the four bag sides and baste along the seamlines to secure. Sew all four sides to construct the bag.

4 Snip notches from each corner seam allowance approximately ¼" (0.5 cm) deep. This is to prevent the fabric from wrinkling. After sewing the four sides, cut off excess allowances to match the ¼" (0.5 cm) notches.

5 Repeat Steps 2–4 to make the bag lining. Turn the bag body inside out so the right side of the fabric is outside and insert the lining wrong side out.

6 For the bag opening: There is a ⅜" (1 cm) difference in height between the bag body and lining because the lining does not have the seam allowance. Fold in the body's seam allowance, and press. Fold over 1½" (4 cm) of the body and lining fabric together and secure the hem with pins.

7 Sew the bag's opening hemline to finish the bag. Press for a clean finish.

8 Determine the leather handles' position by placing them on the bag and marking it with a chalk wedge. Align the stitch line of the opening and the end of the metal buckle.

9 Ready-made leather handles usually have premade stitching holes, but punch the holes with an awl or leather punch to make sure the needle passes through easily.

10 Using a hand-sewing needle and thick thread, hand sew the handles securely to the bag.

11 The finished denim bag. Binding the inside seams with bias tape creates a clean look.

USING BIAS TAPE

The bias is the diagonal line drawn across the weave of the fabric. Thin strips of fabric cut along this diagonal are called bias tape, which is extremely elastic and is used for finishing seams, hemming, and edge finishing.

How to make bias tape

Cut diagonal strips of fabric (oriented 45 degrees to the grain of the fabric). Sew them end-to-end, with the right sides facing together. Trim the fabric that sticks out from the edge. Fold an equal amount of fabric toward the center of the strip and press. Alternatively, bias tape can be folded using a bias-tape maker.

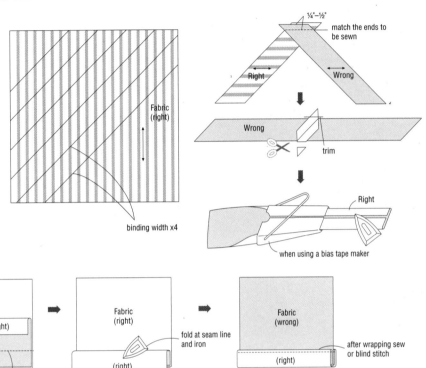

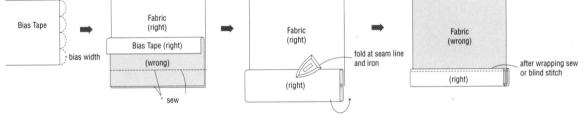

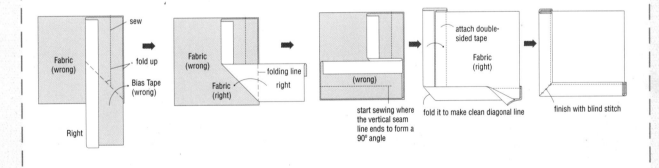

Franc franc

Part 1

Indoor

Refreshing cotton, linen, and gauze skirts and
bags that double as home-décor accents.

Designs by Eun-Joo Cha

Cutting Tips

★ Lay out the pattern and cut the fabric as shown in the illustration. Be sure to place the front panel properly, accommodating the pleats at the center front. ★ Overlock all cut edges. ★ To make the ties, fold in the seam allowances, fold the ties in half lengthwise, and sew.

SEWING INSTRUCTIONS

1 Stitch pin tucks (thin pleats folded and sewn) at the center front. Create the pleats with 6¼" (16 cm) of fabric as shown in the illustration.

2 With the right sides together, sew the front and back panels at the side seams. Press open the side seam allowances.

3 Fold up the hem and sew.

4 With the waist seam allowance, double-fold a ¾" (2 cm) hem and sew.

5 Create the waistband. First, wrap the elastic with leftover skirt fabric. Cut a 1½" (4 cm) -wide strip that is long enough to cover the waistband. Then fold in the seam allowances at both sides and press.

6 Place the elastic band on the inside of the fabric strip and sew the elastic to the waistband. Stretch the elastic slightly while sewing to allow for some ease in the waistband.

7 Place the waistband as shown below and sew it onto the skirt.

8 Fold the waistband inside the garment, tucking under the bottom seam of the band, and sew in place. While sewing, stretch the elastic band steadily to create natural shirring.

9 Embroider the pin-tucks with evenly spaced embroidery stitches.

10 Sew the pocket with straps. Double-fold the seam at the hem toward the right side and sew it in place. Fold the side seams toward the right side and fold over 4¼" (11 cm). Press and sew the sides to create a pocket shape. Attach the ties.

11 Double-fold the top part of the pocket-bag (first fold: ⅜" [1 cm]; second: 1¼" [3 cm]), sew the skirt and pocket-bag together.

01 Gauze Skirt with Pocket

This simple design accentuates the character of embroidered gauze fabric. An elastic waistband adds delicate comfort.

Materials

2 yards (2 m) of embroidered gauze fabric

1½ yards (1.5 m) of ¾" (2 cm) -wide elastic waistband

Embroidery thread

Seam allowances: 1½" (4 cm) each for the hem and waist, ¾" (2 cm) each for the sides, and ⅜" (8 cm) for the center front.

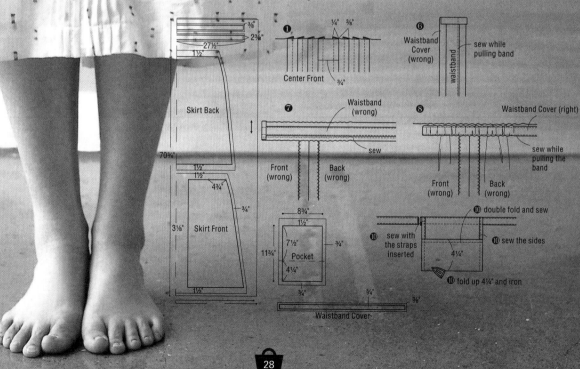

02 Modern Drawstring Bag

This bag's trademark? It can be carried upside-down or right-side up: the bottom and top are identical.

Materials

28" × 17½" (71 × 45 cm) crinkled cotton printed fabric (bag body)

28" × 17½" (71 × 45 cm) solid cotton fabric (lining)

Two 2" (5 cm) squares of denim fabric (for the drawstring cord stops)

1½ yards (150 cm) of ⅝" (1.5 cm) –thick cord

Seam allowances: 1" (2.5 cm) each for top and bottom and ⅝" (1.5 cm) each for the side seams

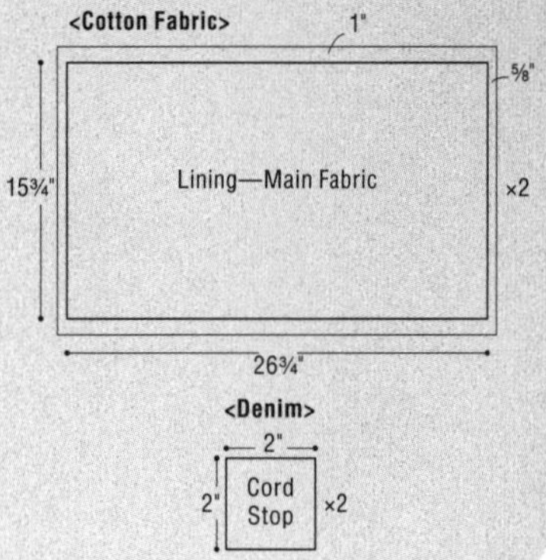

<Cotton Fabric>
1"
⅝"
15¾"
Lining—Main Fabric
×2
26¾"
<Denim>
2"
2"
Cord Stop
×2

Cutting Tips

★ Cut the fabric as shown in the illustration.

SEWING INSTRUCTIONS

1 With right sides together, place the main fabric on top of the lining and pin or baste them. Fold in ¼" (0.5 cm) at the side seams and press. Fold in 1⅜" (1 cm) again at the side seams and pin. Finish side seams by sewing, then pressing.

2 Fold in the top and bottom seams ¼" (0.5 cm) and press. Fold in and press ¼" (2 cm) again. Pin seam in place, then sew, creating the casing for the drawstrings.

3 Fold the stitched fabric in half vertically (toward the main fabric), right sides together. Sew the side seams as shown. Press the seams and turn the bag inside out.

4 Make the cord stops: fold in the top and bottom ⅜" (1 cm) and stitch. Fold the fabric in half and sew two rows of stitches ⅜" (1 cm) apart. The casings will be slightly smaller than the cord so the cord is held snugly.

5 Pin a safety pin to the end of the cord and thread it through the cord stops, following the sequence illustrated below. Tie the ends of the cord together.

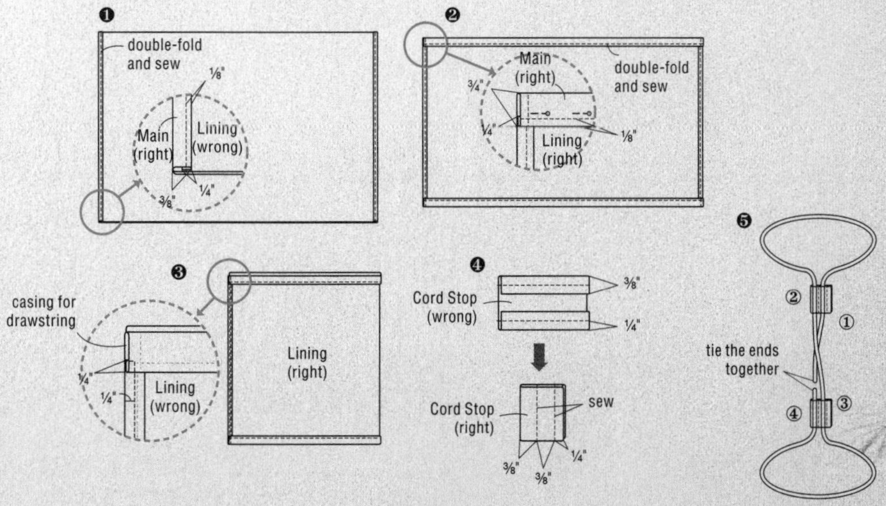

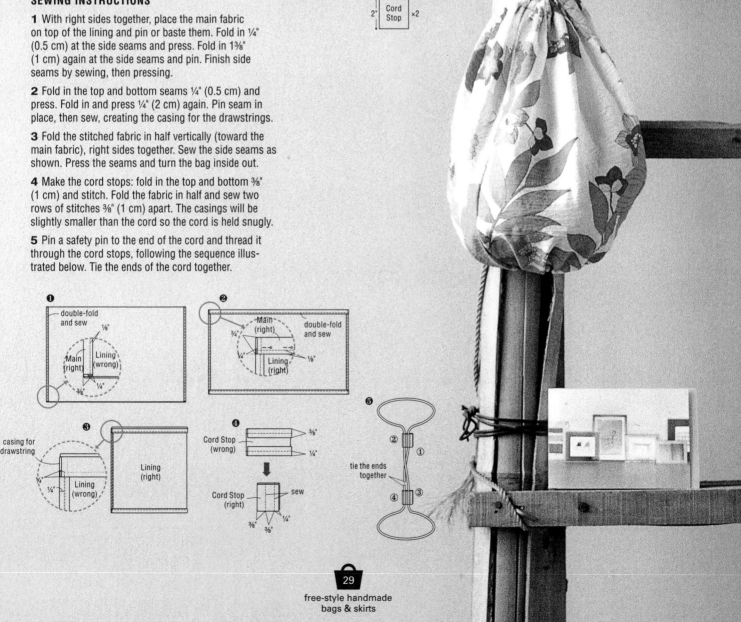

❶
double-fold and sew
⅛"
Main (right)
Lining (wrong)
¼"
⅜"
❷
Main (right)
double-fold and sew
¾"
¼"
⅛"
Lining (right)
❸
casing for drawstring
¼"
¼"
Lining (wrong)
Lining (right)
❹
Cord Stop (wrong)
⅜"
¼"
Cord Stop (right)
sew
⅜"
⅜"
¼"
❺
②
①
tie the ends together
④
③

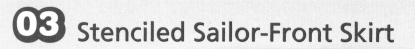

03 Stenciled Sailor-Front Skirt

This skirt features a sailor-front button panel, a unique stitch detail, made from variegated, multicolor thread, and a stenciled, ring-shaped pattern.

04 Quilted Polka-Dot Bag

A perennially cute fabric design is softened around the edges with exposed quilt batting at the handle. This bag is perfect as a gift bag for wine.

Stenciled Sailor-Front Skirt

(shown on page 30)

Materials

59" × 43" (150 × 110 cm) white cotton fabric

Four red buttons

Variegated, multicolor thread

Five to six pieces of fabric-dyeing paper

Seam allowances: ¾" (2 cm) each for the side seams (1½" [4 cm] for the sides where the buttons are attached), 2" (5 cm) for the hem, and ⅜" for the waist.

Cutting Tips

★ Lay out the sample pattern as shown in the illustration and cut out the fabric. ★ Overlock all cut edges.

SEWING INSTRUCTIONS

1 Fold the skirt back darts in half toward the inside and pin them in place. Sew the darts, then press the seams toward the center front.

2 With right sides together, sew the side seams of the center piece and side panels. Do not sew the button-closure opening. Press open the seams.

3 Stitch the skirt front and the skirt back: With right sides together, sew the side seams and press the seams open.

4 With right sides together, sew the two front pieces of the waistband facing to the back waistband facing, making one long strip. Sew the strip to the waist seam with right sides together. Trim off the seam allowance, fold it over, and clean finish both ends. Attach the waistband facing to the center piece of the skirt in the same manner.

5 Press a ⅜" (1 cm) hem. Fold the hem 1½" (4 cm) again and stitch. Topstitch all seams with the thread.

6 Place the buttons as shown in the illustration and mark their positions. Snip buttonholes in the center piece and sew the buttons to each side of the front panel. Finish the buttonholes with a buttonhole stitch.

7 Cut ring shapes from the fabric-dyeing paper and decorate the skirt front (see Tips on page 46).

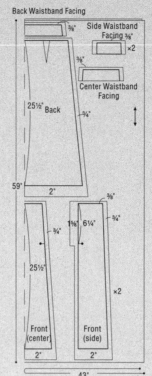

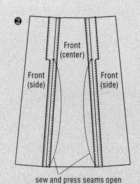

sew and press seams open

Quilted Polka-Dot Bag

(shown on page 31)

Materials

¼ yard (25 cm) pastel polka-dot print quilting fabric

Pink cotton fabric (for the handles)

¼ yard (25 cm) quilt batting

Seam allowance: 2" (5 cm) for the bag opening and ⅜" (1 cm) each for the sides and bottom. (There is no seam allowance for the handle.)

Cutting Tips

★ Cut the printed and pink fabrics as shown in the illustration. ★ Cut the batting the same size as the polka-dot print fabric, except for the bag opening seam allowance (2" [5 cm]).

SEWING INSTRUCTIONS

1 Pin the batting to the wrong side of the polka-dot print fabric. Stitch rows of vertical lines spaced 1½" (4 cm) apart. Stitch the batting to the bottom panel.

2 Stitch the side seams of the polka-dot print fabric, right sides together. Trim ¼" (0.5 cm) from the seam allowances.

3 Pin the bag body to the round bottom and stitch along the seamline. Make snips around the entire seam allowance.

4 For the bag opening seam, fold a ¼" (0.5 cm) hem and press. Fold 1¾" (4.5 cm) again toward the inside and stitch around the opening. Topstitch along the edge of the bag opening.

5 To make the handles, insert the batting between the pink fabric and the polka-dot print fabric. Sew them to the outside of the bag as shown in the illustration. Finish the handle by fraying the edges.

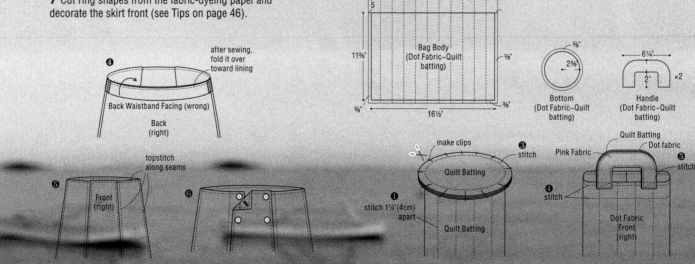

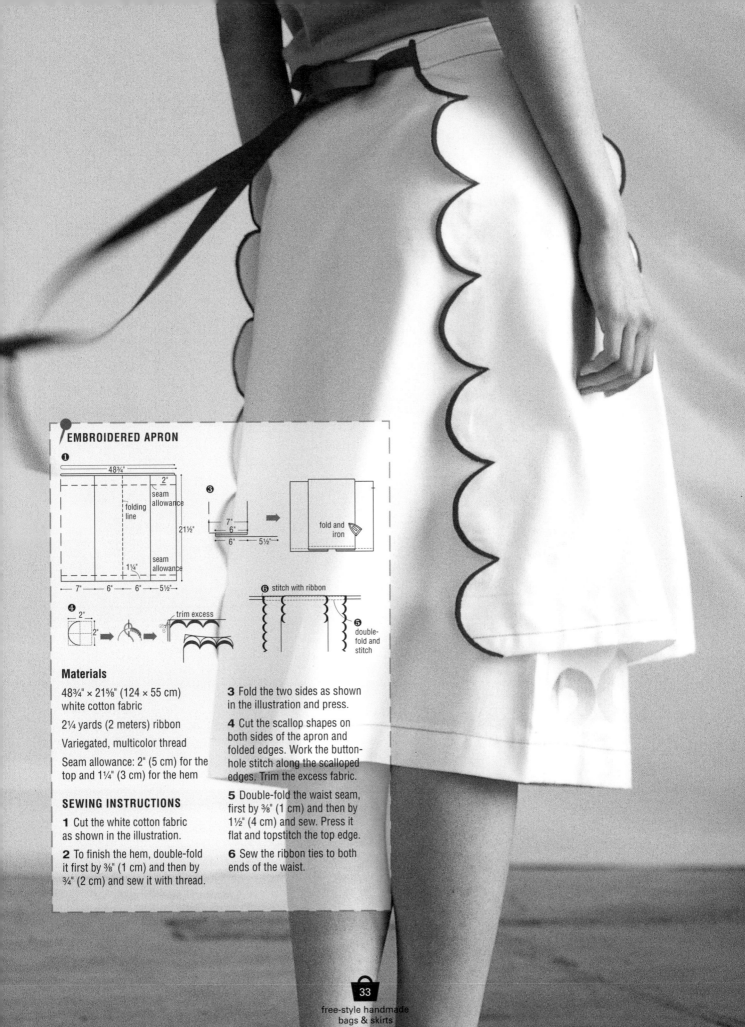

EMBROIDERED APRON

❶

48¾"

2"
seam allowance

folding line

21½"

seam allowance

1¼"

7" — 6" — 6" — 5½"

❸

7"
6"
6" — 5½"

fold and iron

❹

2"

2"

trim excess

❻ stitch with ribbon

❺ double-fold and stitch

Materials

48¾" × 21⅝" (124 × 55 cm) white cotton fabric

2¼ yards (2 meters) ribbon

Variegated, multicolor thread

Seam allowance: 2" (5 cm) for the top and 1¼" (3 cm) for the hem

SEWING INSTRUCTIONS

1 Cut the white cotton fabric as shown in the illustration.

2 To finish the hem, double-fold it first by ⅜" (1 cm) and then by ¾" (2 cm) and sew it with thread.

3 Fold the two sides as shown in the illustration and press.

4 Cut the scallop shapes on both sides of the apron and folded edges. Work the buttonhole stitch along the scalloped edges. Trim the excess fabric.

5 Double-fold the waist seam, first by ⅜" (1 cm) and then by 1½" (4 cm) and sew. Press it flat and topstitch the top edge.

6 Sew the ribbon ties to both ends of the waist.

05 Hand-Painted Denim Bag

A denim handbag is embellished with a freehand
children's-style drawing.

Materials

14½" × 33" (37 × 84 cm) light-colored denim or chambray

Two 14" × 3⅛" (35 × 8 cm) plastic canvas sheets

Embroidery thread

Fabric pastels

Seam allowance: ⅜" (1 cm) for the opening, sides, and handle

Cutting Tips

★ Cut a rectangle as shown in the illustration. Overlock all cut
edges. ★ Cut the plastic canvas to the dimensions indicated
(the canvas provides structure for the handles).

SEWING INSTRUCTIONS

1 Fold a ⅜" (1 cm) seam at the bag opening ends and sew.

2 Cut out two holes for the handles from the center of both bag opening ends (as shown), leaving adequate seam allowance. Clip the curves of the seam allowances and fold them to the wrong side. Center the plastic canvas over the lower handle holes and fold down the inside handle lining. With a needle and embroidery thread, buttonhole stitch around the edge of the handle hole.

3 Fold the bag in half with right sides together and sew the side seams. Turn the bag inside out.

4 With a needle threaded with multiple strands of variegated thread, add a running stitch to the bottom edge of the handle, catching the mesh plastic and fabric lining.

5 Press the finished bag for a clean look.

6 With fabric pastels, draw a design on the bag front. To heat-set the pastel design, place a piece of lightweight fabric over the drawing and press with a hot iron (refer to page 46 for more on fabric dyeing.)

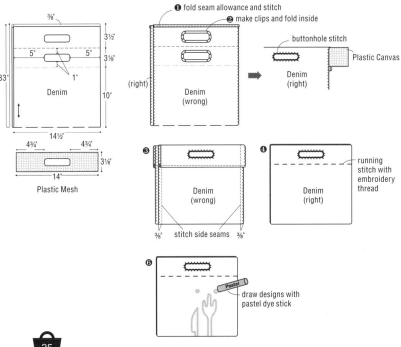

06 Pleated Floral-Print Skirt

This A-line skirt with a front pleat and fitted waist has a formal look, which is offset by the bright, fun print fabric.

Materials

2 yards (2 m) of 45" (110 cm) -wide floral print cotton

Belting (in a length equal to the waist measurement plus 1¼" [3 cm])

One 6" (15 cm) -long invisible zipper

Large hook and eye or bar

Seam allowances: ⅜" (1 cm) for the waist, ¾" (2 cm) for the side seam, and ⅜" (1 cm) for the four sides of the waistband.

Cutting Tips

★ Cut out the pattern as shown in the illustration. Add 2" (5 cm) for the pleats to the front and back pieces. ★ Overlock all cut edges. ★ Transfer the pleat lines to the front and back pieces using a tracing wheel and double-sided chalk paper.

SEWING INSTRUCTIONS

1 Sew together the skirt front and back. Sew the side seams, right sides together, and press the seams open, leaving the seam open for the 6" (15 cm) -long zipper.

2 Create the pleats: Fold 2" (5 cm) pleats as shown in the illustration and press. The front panel has two pleats and the back panel has three.

3 Sew the pleats in place. Sew 6" (15 cm) down from the waist along the folded lines.

4 Insert the zipper into the zipper opening. (Refer to page 54 for how to sew an invisible zipper.)

5 Sew the belt: Refer to steps 8-12 of Making a Basic Skirt, page 22 for complete instructions. The belt end to be attached to the skirt front should be 1¼" (3 cm) longer. Sew the hook to this end.

6 Double-fold the hem (first by ¾" [2 cm] and then by 1¼" [3 cm]) and sew.

37

free-style handmade
bags & skirts

free-style handmade
bags & skirts

07 Reversible Hand-Painted Tote

This handbag, made from oxford and printed cotton fabric, is sturdy and versatile. The dimensions and decorative details can be altered to reflect personal style.

Variation A: Tote Bag

Materials

1 yard (1 m) each white oxford fabric (main fabric) and floral print cotton fabric (lining)

2 yards (2 m) of 1½" (4 cm) -wide webbing

1 piece of plastic canvas, cut to match dimensions of the bag bottom

Fabric paint or dye

Seam allowance: 2⅜" (6.5 cm) for the bag opening and ⅜" (1 cm) for all other seams.

Cutting Tips

★ Cut out the fabric as shown in the illustration. ★ If sewing with lightweight fabric, apply fusible interfacing to the wrong side of the main fabric for added stability (see page 16).

SEWING INSTRUCTIONS

1 On pre-washed and pressed main fabric, paint a design with fabric paint or dye. Press design after it dries (see tips on page 46).

2 Sew the front, back, and bottom pieces of the main fabric, then sew the pieces of the lining fabric. (See steps 2-5 of Making a Basic Bag, page 24.)

3 Turn the main fabric inside out so the right side of the bag is facing out. Nest the lining fabric, right side facing in, within the main fabric.

4 Fold a ⅜" (1 cm) seam allowance on the lining fabric. Fold down another 2" (5 cm) hem and sew hem into place. Topstitch the top edge.

5 Cut two 37½" (95 cm) lengths of webbing for handles. Mark the midpoint of each. Fold each strap in half lengthwise. Sew the strap together along the edges, but only about 2" (5 cm) on either side of the midpoint.

6 Sew each end of the handles about 6¾" (17 cm) from the side seams.

7 Wrap the plastic canvas with a length of unused main fabric and nestle it at the bottom of the bag.

Variation B: Shoulder Bag

Materials

½ yard (0.5 m) each white oxford fabric (main fabric) and floral print cotton fabric (lining)

2 yards (2 m) of 1½" (4 cm) -wide webbing

1 piece of plastic canvas, cut to match dimensions of the bag bottom

Fabric paint or dye

Seam allowance: ⅜" (1 cm) for all seams.

Cutting Tips

★ Cut the fabric as shown in the illustration. ★ The seam allowance of the bag opening is only ⅜" (1 cm), because the webbing will cover the seam.

SEWING INSTRUCTIONS

1 Follow Steps 1–3 from Variation A.

2 Fold and press each seam allowance (both the main fabric and the lining) toward the inside of the bag. Sew along the edges.

3 Place the striped webbing around the bag opening. Pin it in place, then sew the top and bottom edge of the webbing.

4 To create the bag handles, follow Step 5 of Variation A.

5 Position each end of the handles about 4¼" (11 cm) in from the side seams. Sew in place.

6 To finish the bag, follow Step 7 of Variation A.

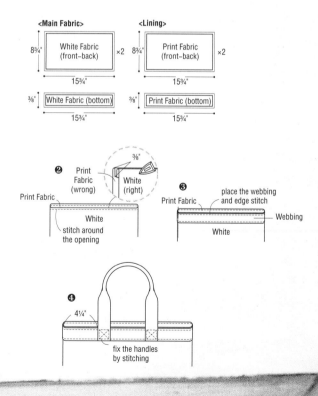

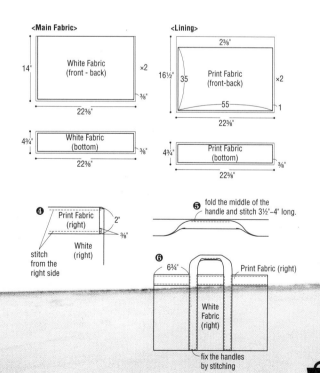

08 Vintage-Style Long Skirt with Pockets

This cargo skirt is made from two panels of straight, striped fabric and embellished with oversized pockets.

Materials

2 yards (2 m) of striped linen

Small piece of denim

2½ yards (2.5 m) of ⅜" (1 cm) -wide elastic band for the waist and hem

2 plastic cord locks

Fusible interfacing

Red sewing thread

Seam allowance: 1¼" (3 cm) for the waist, ¾" (2 cm) for the sides, and 1½" (4 cm) for the hem. Refer to the pattern illustration for the pocket seam allowance.

Cutting Tips

★ Cut out the fabric as shown in the illustration.
★ Following the illustration at right, apply fusible interfacing to the gray area of the denim pocket flap.
★ Overlock all cut edges. ★ Cut elastic in half.

SEWING INSTRUCTIONS

1 With right sides together, sew the front and back skirt panels together along the seamline. Press seams open and leave the slit folded.

2 Fold in the hem ⅜" (1 cm) and press. After folding another 1¼" (3 cm) hem, sew the hem.

3 Leaving enough room for the elastic casing, topstitch along the slit edge.

4 Line up the denim and striped fabric as shown in the illustration and create two pockets and two pocket flaps.

5 Sew the pockets: Pin the bottom of the pocket ¾" (2 cm) above the top of the slit. Fold the side and bottom seam allowances ⅜" (1 cm) inside and sew the pocket to the skirt with colored thread.

6 For the denim flaps, fold the seam allowance inside and sew them to the skirt.

7 Fold down the ⅜" (1 cm) waist seam allowance, then fold down the waist again another ⅜" (2 cm). Sew along the waistline. Snip two holes at the skirt front (inside the waist) and thread one elastic through the waist casing and the other through the hem casing. Thread the ends of the elastic through cord lock and cinch the ends.

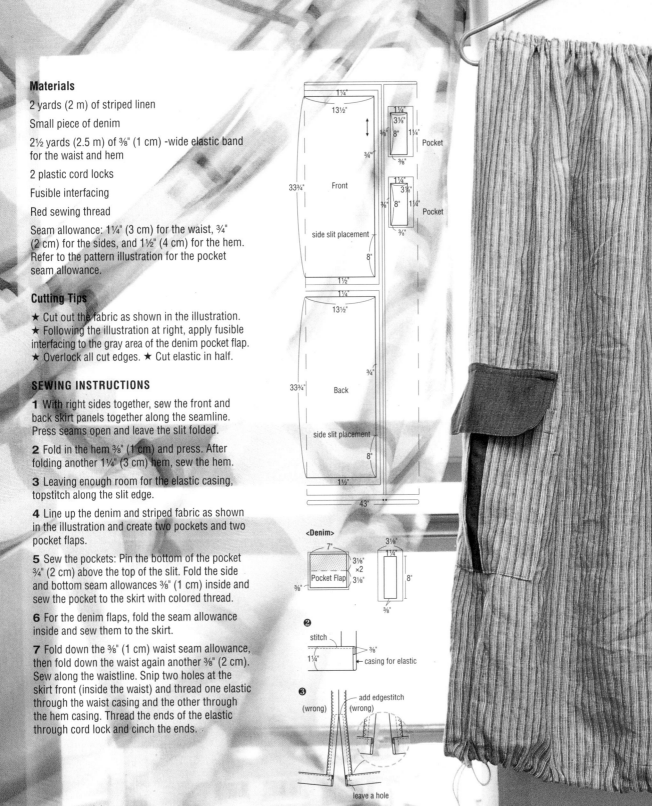

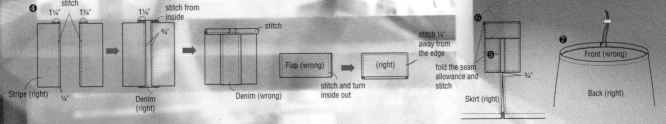

Materials

1 yard (1 m) each of three different printed, heavyweight cotton fabrics

Synthetic leather handles

Ribbon (sturdy enough for bag handles)

Seam allowance for the bag sides is ¼" (0.5 cm) and 1" (2.5 cm) for the opening.

Cutting Tips

★ Cut out the fabric as shown in the illustration. The measurements for large, medium, and small bags are labeled a, b, and c. ★ Each bag's depth can be adjusted to suit different tastes. ★ If the cotton fabric is prone to fraying, overlock the edges.

SEWING INSTRUCTIONS

1 With right sides together, fold the fabric in half and sew the side seams.

2 Square the bag bottoms by folding the bottom corners as shown in the illustration. Sew along the edges.

3 Fold the seam allowance of the bag opening and sew all around.

4 Attach the handles: For bag a, attach the synthetic leather handle by securely sewing the end of the loop to the bag. For bag b, cut two equal lengths of leather ribbon and sew the ends directly to outside of the bag opening. For bag c, punch two holes at the four corners of the bag opening. Cut two equal lengths of leather ribbon, thread the ribbon ends through the holes, and knot the ends to secure. Optional: Insert eyelets into the punched holes for additional stability and a finished look.

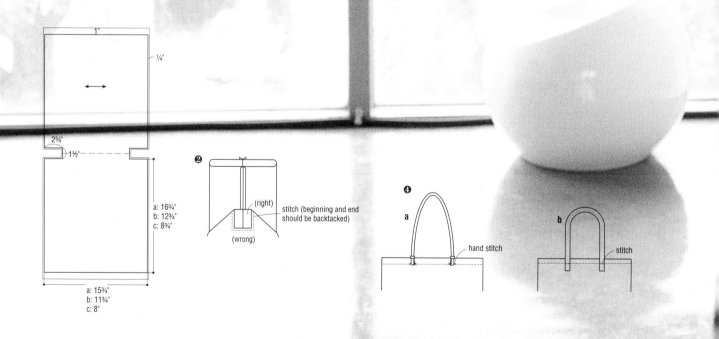

1"

¼"

2¾"

1½"

a: 16¾"
b: 12¾"
c: 8¾"

a: 15¾"
b: 11¾"
c: 8"

❷

(right)

stitch (beginning and end should be backtacked)

(wrong)

❹

a

hand stitch

b

stitch

c

thread the ribbon through holes

09 Basket Bags with Leather Handles

These multipurpose bags can be used for storage or as accessories. Their durable construction makes them ideally suited for both stowing *and* toting.

Skirts and bags—handmade or store-bought—can be dyed and decorated with a number of tools and products. These common items can be found in most art, craft, sewing, or even paper-arts stores.

FABRIC PASTELS

These permanent dye sticks can be used on cotton T-shirts, bags, upholstery items such as curtains and pillowcases, and more. White or light-colored cotton, wool, and silk fabrics are the best bases for fabric pastels.

FABRIC-PAINTING PEN

This pen-shaped dyeing tool is ideal for drawing fine lines and well suited for cotton and linen fabric. Like most fabric paint, the paint must be pressed or placed in a dryer after it has dried to heat-set (or make permanent) the design.

FABRIC-DYEING PAINT

This paint is specially formulated for painting on fibers and can be used on any fabric surface. When painting, always place thick paper, cardboard, or other protective surface underneath the fabric and between fabric layers to avoid the paint seeping or bleeding through and staining the fabric underneath. After the paint dries, cover it with a piece of thin fabric or paper and press it for 1-2 minutes to heat-set the paint. The paint can be brushed, stamped, stenciled, or applied in many ways.

Instructions for Fabric Dyeing

1. Fabrics that wrinkle easily should be pulled taut and pinned. Draw the design on the fabric with the dye.

2 A design can be painted freehand, or a stencil can be created from thin, clear plastic.

3 Layer lightweight fabric on top of the paint and press it at high heat. The paint is now permanent and washable.

FABRIC-DYEING PAPER

This heat-set dyeing paper dyes cotton fabric and synthetics instantly. Place the fabric to be dyed on the ironing board. Cut the dyeing paper to the desired shape(s) and place the paper on top of the fabric. Press with an iron for 10-15 seconds. (Layering multiple sheets and colors of paper creates endless design possibilities.)

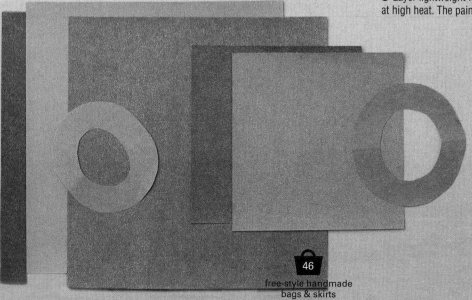

Designer Profile: Eun-Joo Cha

Eun-Joo Cha is a fashion stylist and merchandiser who works for a number of clients, including fashion magazines and advertising agencies. She studied clothing design in college, and she has been widely recognized for her DIY-inspired fashion sense. She has written several books about fashion accessories. While she designs natural, casual styles with an eye for comfort and practicality, her use of unique textiles and simple dyeing techniques are her trademarks.

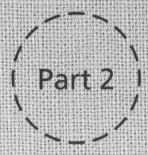

Part 2

Downtown

These unique, embellished designs are unlike any found everyday boutiques. The novel surface details and clever constructions are sure to sparkle outdoors in the sun or in the bright lights of the big city!

Designs by Rhang Lee

10 Appliqué Bag with Wooden Handles

This piece is defined by its freestyle, beaded, patchwork design. Its simple construction is derived from a simple rectangle.

Materials

Two pieces 27½" × 21½" (70 × 65 cm) heavyweight cotton fabric (one for main fabric, one for lining)

1 pair of 11" (28 cm) wooden handles

Embellishment materials (beads, sequins, yarn, small pieces of fabric)

Embroidery thread

Seam allowance: 2¾" (7 cm) for the opening and ⅝" (1.5 cm) for the side seams.

Cutting Tips

★ Cut each fabric rectangle into two panels, as shown in the illustration. ★ ⅝" (1.5 cm) of the seam allowance for the top is allotted for the actual seam and the remainder is for wrapping around the handle. ★ If using a heavyweight fabric, change the machine needle to size 14.

SEWING INSTRUCTIONS

1 Make the basic shape of the bag: Layer the main and lining fabrics with wrong sides together. Fold the layered fabric in half with the right side of the lining facing outwards. Press the bottom of the bag. Sew the side seams, leaving 2" (5 cm) from the top open, finishing the ends of the seamline with a reverse stitch.

2 Trim a small triangle from the corner of the seam allowance. Press the seams open. Double-fold the trimmed seam allowance and the side seam allowance, then hemstitch the seams.

3 Fold and press the ⅝" (1.5 cm) seam allowance for the bag opening on both the main and lining fabrics.

4 Baste the bottom part of the seam created in step 3. Gently pull the thread to gather the fabric to the width of the bag handles.

5 Insert the top edge of the bag opening through the slot of the bag handle. Wrap the remaining seam allowance around the handle and hemstitch it to the inside of the bag using white thread. Remove the basting thread from step 4.

6 Embellish the outside of the bag front and back with embroidery thread, adding beads and sequins, couching yarn, and appliquéing small pieces of fabric.

Main Fabric Lining ×2

2¾" 25½" ⅝" 27½"

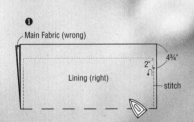

❶ Main Fabric (wrong) / Lining (right) / 4¾" / 2" / stitch

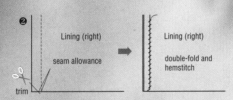

❷ Lining (right) / seam allowance / trim → Lining (right) / double-fold and hemstitch

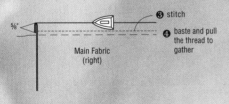

❸ stitch / ⅝" / ❹ baste and pull the thread to gather / Main Fabric (right)

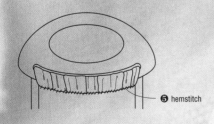

❺ hemstitch

11 Beaded Denim Skirt

This classic A-line denim skirt design is embellished with a strip of vibrant print fabric. Adding beaded fringe to the hemline evokes an exotic air.

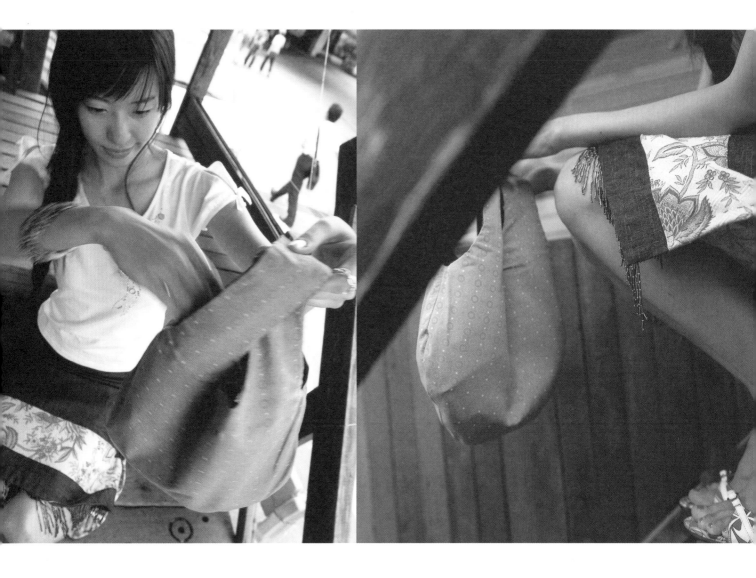

12 Reversible Ethnic-Style Bag

This sublimely simple construction, designed to coordinate with the Beaded Denim Skirt, features a body and handle from one continuous length of fabric.

Beaded Denim Skirt

(shown on page 52)

Materials

1½ yards (1.5 m) of 36" (90 cm) -wide denim fabric

1⅛ yards (1.1 m) of printed fabric (contrast stripe)

1¼ yards (1.2 m) of beaded fringe

8" (20 cm) -long invisible zipper

Embroidery thread (red)

Seam allowance: 2" (5 cm) for the hem, ⅝" (1.5 cm) for the side seams (including 2¾" [7 cm] for the slit), and ⅜" (1 cm) each for all other seams.

Cutting Tips

★ Cut out the sample pattern as shown in the illustration. If using fabric that is 60" (150 cm), only use 1 yard (1 m): fold the fabric from both sides toward the center then cut out the pattern. ★ Overlock all cut edges. ★ Folding the front and back darts toward the inside and pin them in place. Sew all darts. ★ Fold and press the seam allowance of the contrast fabric.

<Denim>

⅜"
⅝"
Front
slit   5"   2¾"
2"
65"
⅜"
⅝"
Back
Slit   5"   2¾"
2"
35½"

<Print>

⅜"
Front   2¾"
15¾"
Back   2¾"
35½"

Inserting an invisible zipper

The teeth of invisible zippers are covered by the zipper tape. When pressed, ¼" (0.5 cm) of extra space will remain on each side of the zipper tape. Invisible zippers are commonly used for skirts and dresses, since the zipper's seamline does not show on the outside of the garment. The invisible zipper can be sewn using a one-toe pressure foot as shown in the illustration. (If a specialty invisible-zipper foot is used, pressing is not necessary.)

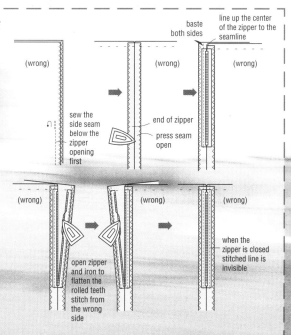

(wrong)

sew the side seam below the zipper opening first

end of zipper

press seam open

baste both sides

line up the center of the zipper to the seamline

(wrong)

(wrong)

(wrong)

(wrong)

(wrong)

open zipper and iron to flatten the rolled teeth stitch from the wrong side

when the zipper is closed stitched line is invisible

SEWING INSTRUCTIONS

1 Lay the contrast fabric strips on the front and back, aligned with the top of the slit. Sew the top and bottom of each strip, using thread in a color that matches the contrast fabric.

2 Sew each side seam of the skirt. For the left side seam, leave sufficient length at the top for inserting the zipper. Press the seams open.

3 For the slit, fold the seam allowances from the side seamline. Fold ⅜" (1 cm) from the ends of the seam allowance, then hemstitch both edges. Also, hemstitch the rest of the side seam allowances.

4 Attach the invisible zipper (refer to instructions on the previous page).

5 Fold over and press the waist seamline. Neaten the waist seam allowance with a catchstitch.

6 Fold up and press ¾" (2 cm) of the hem seam allowance. Fold up 1¼" (3 cm) again and press. If adding the beaded fringe to the hem, pin and sew it in place along the hemline before the second hem is turned. The stitching along the hem will not show from the outside of the garment.

7 Blind stitch the hem seam allowance.

8 Embellish the bottom of the skirt with a running stitch.

Reversible Ethnic-Style Bag
(shown on page 53)

Materials

Two 15¾" × 19¾" (40 × 50 cm) pieces denim fabric (main fabric)

Two 15¾" × 19¾" (40 × 50 cm) pieces printed cotton fabric (lining)

Two 14¾" × 5" (37.5 × 13 cm) pieces printed fabric (contrast stripe)

Seam allowances: ⅝"(1.5 cm) for the top of the handle, ⅜" (1 cm) for the curved seams, and ⅝" (1.5 cm) for the contrast stripe.

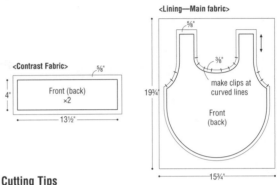

Cutting Tips

★ Using the sample pattern, cut out the bag front and back for a total of four pieces. Add ¼" (0.5 cm)-long snips to the curved seam allowances. ★ All seam allowances for the contrast stripe should be folded and pressed.

SEWING INSTRUCTIONS

1 Sew the contrast stripe to the right side of each main fabric. Make sure the sides of the contrasting fabric stripe are aligned.

2 With right sides of the main fabric together, sew the top edges of the handles and the bottom part of the bag. Press the seam open.

3 Prepare the lining in the same manner as the main fabric in step 2.

4 For the main and lining fabrics, fold the curved, snipped seam allowance of the handle and press.

5 Insert the lining inside the main fabric, wrong sides together. Aligning all edges perfectly, pin the edges of the handle.

6 Blind stitch the main fabric and lining along the edges.

7 Press the bag. Add a few tack stitches to the bottom of the bag to hold the lining and main fabric together.

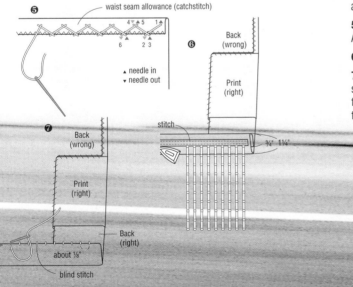

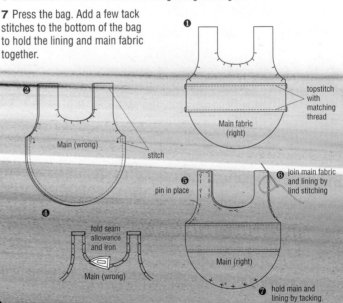

13 Reversible Wrap Skirt and Top

This layered, reversible wrap skirt features pin-tucked details that assure a refined fit to your figure. The skirt also doubles as a top.

Materials

1 yard (1 m) of 60" (1.5 m) -wide cotton fabric

Lightweight fusible interfacing

Three or four colors of embroidery thread

Embroidery needle

Seam allowances: ⅜" (1 cm) for all seams (the skirt piece does not have any seam allowance)

Cutting Tips

★ Cut out the fabric as shown in the illustration. Because the length of the belt is determined by the number of pin-tucks, cut the tie fabric only after step 2. ★ Prepare the belt ties by folding the seam allowances inside and pressing them.

SEWING INSTRUCTIONS

1 Fray the edges of the skirt. Sew ⅛" (0.3 cm) away from three edges of the skirt, so fraying is minimized.

2 Sew the pin-tucks: Irregular, asymmetrical pin-tucks can be spaced ½" (1 cm) to 2" (5 cm) apart. Thirty-four pin-tucks are included here.

3 Cut the waistband fabric, matching its length to the length of the waist in step 2. Pin interfacing to one side of the waistband.

4 Fold the waistband in half lengthwise. Fold all seam allowances to the inside and press.

5 Sew the waistband to the skirt: Place the belt along the waistline, pin it in place, then sew along the waistline.

6 Sew the belt ties. Place the ties so that the sewn side faces up. Insert the ties into each side of the waistband and sew in place.

7 Embroider a design on one side of the waistband.

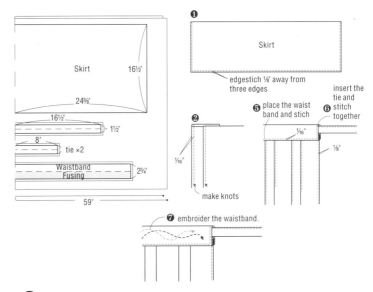

14 Backpack and Messenger Bag

The backpack and messenger bag are made from the same fabric and embellishments. The front pocket is detachable so two different looks can be created with one bag.

free-style handmade
bags & skirts

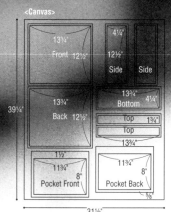

‹Canvas›

- Front 13¾" × 12½"
- Side 4¼" × 12½"
- Side
- Back 13¾" × 12½"
- Bottom 13¾" × 4¼"
- Top 13¾"
- Top
- 13¾"
- Pocket Front 1½" / 11¾" × 8"
- Pocket Back 11¾" × 8"
- 5⁄8"
- 39¼"
- 31½"

‹Print›

- Front 13¾" × 12½"
- side 4¼" × 12½"
- side
- Back 13¾" × 12½"
- Bottom 13¾" × 4¼"
- 27½"
- 31½"

Square Backpack with Button Embellishments
(shown on page 58)

Materials

31½" × 39¼" (80 × 100 cm) canvas fabric (main fabric)

31½" × 27½" (80 × 70 cm) printed cotton fabric (lining)

31½" × 27½" (80 × 70 cm) fusible interfacing

1½" (4 cm) -wide webbing (two 24⅜" [62 cm] pieces for shoulder straps and two 14½" [37 cm] pieces for handles)

13¾" (35 cm) -long zipper, 1¼" (3 cm) wide

Embellishments (buttons, snaps, hooks, safety pins, thread, and glue)

Bias tape

Seam allowances: ⅜" (1 cm) for the bag body, 1½" (4 cm) for the top seam of the pocket, and ⅝" (1.5 cm) for the pocket sides and bottom.

Cutting Tips

★ Cut out the pattern (except the top part of the lining) as shown in the illustration
★ The fusible interfacing measurements are the same as the main fabric. Cut the fusible interfacing and press the pieces to the main fabric (except the top part of the lining).

SEWING INSTRUCTIONS

1 Fold and press the seam allowances for the top edge of the bag. Pin the zipper to the fabric from inside the seam allowance (refer to illustration 2).

2 Center the webbing in the top edge of the bag, shape the handles and pin in place, then box stitch the ends.

3 With right sides together, sew the front, side, back, and bottom of the bag. When sewing the back panel to the top and bottom panels, pin the shoulder straps in place within the seam, then sew them together. Trim any excess fusible interfacing from the seam allowances. Wrap the seam allowances with bias tape and sew along the base of the tape to finish.

4 To make the bag lining, sew each lining panel in the same manner as step 3. Fold and press the seam allowance of the bag opening.

5 Turn the main bag inside out so the right side faces out and insert the lining. Shape the bag by aligning all corners. Blind stitch the top edge of the lining to the main fabric.

6 Make the pocket: For the opening, double-fold the seam allowance and sew. Edge stitch the pocket opening edge. With right sides together, sew the sides and the bottom. Turn the pocket inside out and edge stitch the seams. Sew the snaps at the four corners of the reverse side.

7 Sew the snaps to the front of the bag, matching the snaps' position to the pocket.

8 Glue the buttons, snaps, hooks, and other materials into place and sew them with colored threads. (Refer to page 120 for more information on attaching embellishments.)

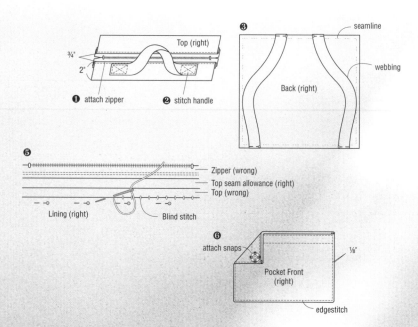

❶ attach zipper   ❷ stitch handle

❸ seamline / webbing / Back (right) / Top (right) / ¾" / 2"

❺ Zipper (wrong) / Top seam allowance (right) / Top (wrong) / Lining (right) / Blind stitch

❻ attach snaps / Pocket Front (right) / ⅛" / edgestitch

Messenger Bag with Button Embellishments

(shown on page 59)

Materials

15¾" × 21½" (40 × 55 cm) brown canvas fabric

45¼" (115 cm) -long and 1½" (4 cm) -wide piece of webbing

13¾" (35 cm) -long and 1¼" (3 cm) -wide zipper (metal teeth)

Bias tape

Embellishments (buttons, snaps, hooks, safety pins, thread, and glue)

Seam allowances: 1" (2.5 cm) for all seams.

Cutting Tips

★ Cut the fabric following the measurements above. ★ Since the seam allowance is wide, the bias tape should be wide as well. Bias tape can be customized to the desired width (refer to page 25). ★ Find a metal zipper that is already cut to the correct length, since it is hard to cut a metal tooth zipper with basic sewing tools. ★ Use a machine needle that is sized for your fabric.

SEWING INSTRUCTIONS

1 Fold and press each seam allowance for the front and back of the bag opening. Pin the webbing to the right side of the zipper.

2 Attach the zipper: Position the right side of the zipper on the fabric's right side and sew from the inside of the seam allowance. Turn the fabric over and edge stitch from the right side. Repeat for the opposite side. The straps will be sewn together at the same time.

3 Wrap the seam allowances with bias tape and sew along the base of the tape to finish.

4 Pin the front and back panels, with right sides together. Sew along the side seams and bottom. Adding another row of stitching outside the first seamline will reinforce the seam. Finish the seam allowances with bias tape.

5 Embellish the front of the bag: Glue the buttons, snaps, hooks, and other materials into place and sew them with colored threads. (Refer to page 120 for more information on attaching embellishments.)

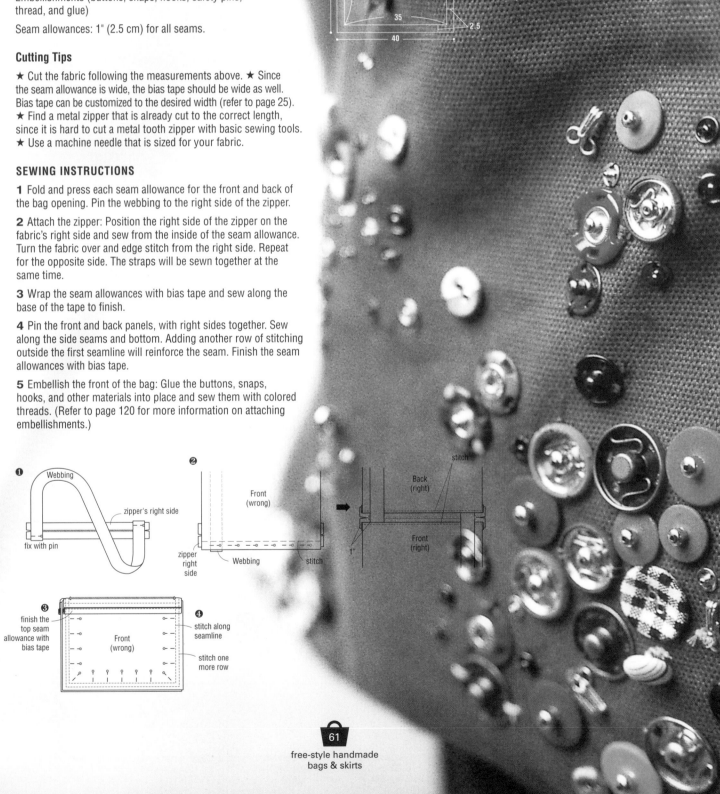

15 Avant-Garde Yoke Skirt

This playful knee-length skirt features a frayed and exposed yoke seam.

16 Basic Yoke Skirt

This above-the-knee skirt with a rounded yoke flatters and slims the waist.

Materials

2 yards (2 m) of 45" (110 cm) -wide cotton fabric

One 6" (15 cm) -long invisible zipper

Seam allowances: 2" (5 cm) for the hem, ⅝" (1.5 cm) for the side seams, and ¾" (1 cm) for the waistline and yoke.

Cutting Tips

★ Cut the sample pattern as shown in the illustration. ★ Overlock all cut edges. ★ Baste along the top edge of the skirt front and back, then pull the thread to gather the fabric. Be sure to gather the skirt fabric so it matches the seam length of the yoke bottom.

Basic Yoke Skirt

SEWING INSTRUCTIONS

1 With right sides together, sew the yoke and yoke facing into the front and back panels.

2 Align the front and back panels and sew the yoke side seams, matching the seamline. Leave room in the seam along the wearer's left side for the zipper. Clip along the bottom curved seam allowance of the yoke. Fold seam allowances to the inside and press.

3 From inside the yoke, sew the seam allowance of the yoke to the yoke facing 1/16" (0.2 cm) away from the waistline. This is to secure the seam allowance as well as to keep the yoke facing in place. Turn it inside out after sewing.

4 With right sides together, sew the side seams of the skirt. (On the left side, start sewing below the zipper opening.) Press the seams open.

5 Pin the front yoke to the gathered skirt and sew along the seamline. For the yoke facing, fold the seam allowance inside and secure it with a blind stitch.

6 Press open the zipper opening seam allowance. Attach the zipper (refer to page 50 for instructions on inserting an invisible zipper).

7 Double-fold the hem and blind stitch the hem to finish. Press the skirt.

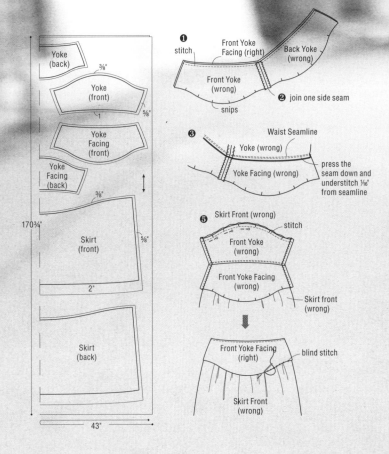

Avant-Garde Yoke Skirt

(shown on page 62)

Materials

2¼ yards (2 m) of 45" (110 cm) -wide cotton fabric

6" (15 cm) -long invisible zipper

Colored thread

Sequin trim

Seam allowances: 2" (5 cm) for the hem, ⅝" (1.5 cm) for the side seams, and ¾" (1 cm) for the waistline and yoke.

Cutting Tips

★ The pattern placement is the same as the Basic Yoke Skirt. Use the longer front and back skirt patterns.
★ The length of the yoke seam allowance can be adjusted as desired since it will be exposed. ★ After gathering the top edge of the skirt, sew along the gathered waistline to anchor the gathers. ★ Make ribbon embellishments with the leftover fabric. Cut several strips of fabric in different lengths and fray the edges.

SEWING INSTRUCTIONS

1 Follow steps 1-3 for the Basic Yoke Skirt, however, overlock the bottom yoke seam and do not make snips in the curved seam allowance.

2 Sew the side seams of the skirt front and back. Sew the seams with the wrong sides together so that the seam allowances are visible on the outside of the skirt.

3 Align and overlap the top edge of the skirt and bottom of the yoke and pin in place. Sew the seam so it is visible from the outside of the skirt.

4 Insert the invisible zipper into the side seam. Note that the skirt does not have the zipper opening seam allowance inside the skirt.

5 Topstitch around the skirt ¾" (1 cm) above the hem. Fray the edge of the hem. Fray the edges of the sides and yoke seam as well.

6 Using colored thread, baste the ribbons to the outside of the skirt. Sew the sequin trim to some of the ribbons to embellish further. (Refer to page 127 for how to attach sequin trim.)

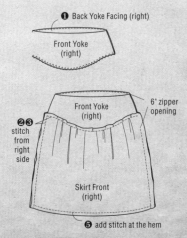

Tips: Embellishment and Trims

Adding embellishments, notions, and trims is a perfect way to personalize a bag, skirt, or any other garment and accessory.

1 Iron-on appliqué

2 Fabric-covered buttons (used in Backpack and Messenger Bag, page 58)

3 Plastic and faux wood buttons

4 Beaded fringe (used in Beaded Denim Skirt, page 52)

5 Sequin trim (used in Avant-Garde Yoke Skirt, page 62)

6 Neon vinyl ribbon (used in Milky White Handbag, page 72)

7 ⅝"(1.5 cm) -wide grosgrain ribbon with water droplet pattern

8 ⅜" (1 cm) -wide grosgrain ribbon with camouflage pattern

9 1" (2.5 cm) -wide striped grosgrain ribbon

10 ⅝" (1.5 cm) -wide ribbon with embroidered clovers and ladybugs

11 ⅜" (1 cm) -wide woven trim with camouflage pattern

12 1¼" (3 cm) -wide woven rainbow trim

13 ⅜" (1 cm) -wide embroidered ribbon

14 ⅜" (1 cm) -wide embroidered ribbon with floral motif

15 Embroidered fringe

16 Black and silver scrolling sequin trim

Designer Profile: Rhang Lee

Rhang Lee is a runway fashion stylist who majored in fashion design. She is now an active member of the Model Center for major fashion shows, including the Seoul Collection, S.F.A.A., Prêt-à-Porter Busan, and Preview in Shanghai. Her designs harmonize simple materials with detailed handiwork. In particular, she suggests novel uses for hand embellishments, such as beads, buttons, and hand stitching, that anyone can freely personlize.

Milky White Handbag

Appliqué Bag with
Wooden Handles

Messenger Bag

Hand-Drawn
Denim Bag

what's your style?

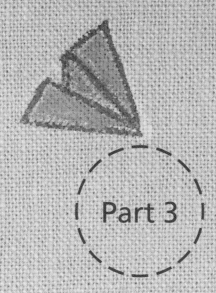

Part 3

Outdoors

These bags are custom-built for practicality and these skirts
are the essence of comfort. Together, these pieces will enhance
any long-awaited, fresh-air getaway.

Designs by Hyo-Sun Jang

17 Milky White Handbag

This bag is constructed with creamy white synthetic rubber-like fabric and a band of water-droplet print fabric. Clear plastic handles complete the fun, functional look.

Materials

15½" × 24¼" (40 × 62 cm) white synthetic rubber-like fabric

Two 4" × 4" (10 × 10 cm) squares of fabric (handle loops)

15½" × 6¼" (40 × 16 cm) polyester water-droplet print fabric

One pair of 6" (15 cm) -wide clear plastic handles

Two 15" (38 cm) -long and ¾" - 1¼" (2-3 cm) -wide neon vinyl tapes

White bias tape

White sewing thread

Fishing line

Double-sided tape

Seam allowances: ⅜" (1 cm) for all seams.

Cutting Tips

★ Cut the body and handle loops as shown in the illustration. Leave ⅜" (1 cm) only at the side seam allowances for the body of the bag. ★ Cut the fabric for the pocket, creating a ⅜" (1 cm) seam allowances all around. Fold and sew the seam allowance of the top edge. ★ Because of the thickness of the rubber fabric, use a size 16 machine needle and thick thread, such as size 30 polyester thread. Sew slowly. If this fabric proves too cumbersome to handle, a lighter vinyl fabric can be substituted.

SEWING INSTRUCTIONS

1 Center the water-droplet fabric at the front center and use double-sided tape to hold the fabric in place. Sew along the bottom of the fabric, then sew three vertical lines to create four pockets (as shown in the illustration).

2 Place the handle loop inside the bag opening and sew ¼" (0.5 cm) down from the edge. Sew the second loop.

3 Sew the vinyl tape around the edge of the bag opening.

4 With right sides together, sew the side seams.

5 Bind the side seams with white bias tape.

6 Shape the bottom corners of the bag as shown in the illustration and sew in place. Hem stitch the bottom.

7 Turn the entire bag inside out. (The thickness of the fabric might make it challenging.)

8 Place the plastic ring handles over the handle loop fabric and fold the loop in half, wrapping it around the handle. Sew the loop to secure it to the bag body.

9 Tack stitch the loop and the outside fabric with clear fishing line (so the stitches will not show).

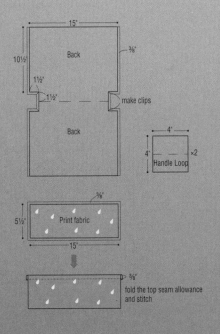

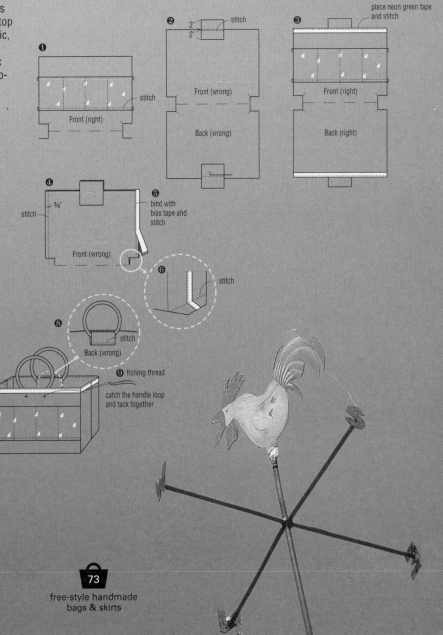

Pocket

³⁄₈"

1½"

2¾"

3½"

9⅜"

³⁄₈"

Main fabric lining

2¾"

5¼"

2¾"   4"   4"

10⅝"

Materials

11½" × 6" (29 × 15.5 cm) water-droplet print fabric (main fabric)

11½" × 6" (29 × 15.5 cm) ivory oxford fabric (lining)

4½" × 3½" (11 × 9 cm) piece of ivory oxford (pocket)

Additional water-droplet print fabric (bias tape)

23⅜" (60 cm) -long yellow vinyl ribbon

5½" (14 cm) -long and ¾" (2 cm) -wide light blue cotton tape

Bias tape

Seam allowances: ⅜" (1 cm) for all seams.

Cutting Tips

★ Cut the fabric as shown in the illustration.
★ Sew along one cut end of the cotton tape to prevent fraying (since one end will be exposed).

18 Traveler's Case

This wallet-style organizer is ideal for toting a passport or maps. Its simple construction lends itself to experimentation with various fabrics, shapes, and functions.

SEWING INSTRUCTIONS

1 With right sides together, sew three sides of the seamline. Turn fabric inside out through the open side and press.

2 Topstitch ¼" (0.5 cm) from the outside around the edge *on three sides only*.

3 Press the folded side and sew the top and bottom, echo-stitching the sewn line so the seams overlap.

4 Make ¾" (2 cm) -wide bias tape with water-droplet print fabric (see page 25). Fold the top seam allowance of the pocket, wrap it with half-folded bias tape, and sew in place. Fold the left side seam allowance and sew. Fold and press the bottom and right side seam allowances.

5 Fold the right side seam allowance inside and align the ¾" (2 cm) -wide light blue cotton tape on top of the seam. Sew it to the main fabric. Insert the yellow vinyl ribbon at the center of the right side during sewing, continuing to sew the seamline.

6 Sew the pocket to the wallet as shown in the illustration. Trim the excess seam allowance.

7 Fold the pocket and sew the bottom edge, noting that the stitch line should overlap. Fold the case in half and wrap it with the ribbon straps. Binding the top and bottom of the travel wallet can add a nice decorative effect.

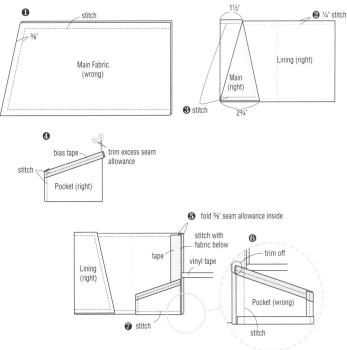

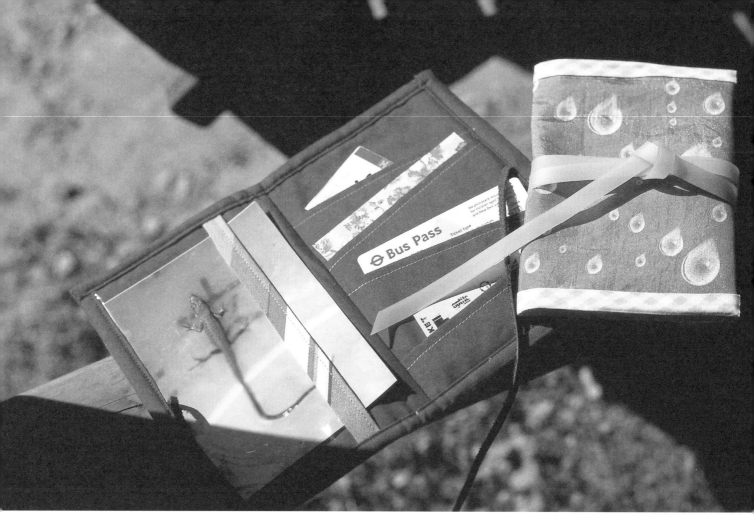

Variation B:
Zigzag Pocket Wallet

Materials

One 9⅜" × 7½" (24 × 19 cm) piece of print fabric (main fabric)

One 10" × 7½" (25 × 19 cm) piece of solid fabric (lining)

One 5" × 15¾" (12.5 × 40 cm) piece of solid fabric (four pockets)

One 4" × 7½" (10 × 19 cm) piece of vinyl

¾" (2 cm) -wide bias tape in two different colors (solid and print)

Leather strap

Seam allowances: ⅜" (1 cm) for all seams.

Cutting Tips

★ Cut the fabric as shown in the illustration.
★ Wrap one edge of the vinyl with bias tape and sew in place. ★ Fold each top edge of pockets ⅜" (1 cm) and sew in place. Trim the excess seam allowance.

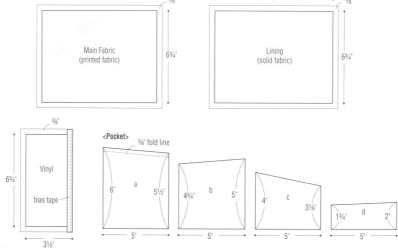

SEWING INSTRUCTIONS

1 Cut the lining fabric in half and arrange the plastic sheet and the pockets as shown in the illustration. Baste the edges.

2 With the pocket sides facing each other, sew the center. Iron the seam toward one side.

3 With right sides together, sew the lining and main fabric along three sides. Turn fabric inside out. Snip each corner seam allowance.

4 Fold the seam allowance of the open side to the inside and sew along the edges from the outside.

5 Bind all four sides of the wallet with bias tape. (Refer to page 25 for instructions on binding the corners.) Insert, center, and sew the leather ties in place along the outside edges of the wallet while sewing the bias tape.

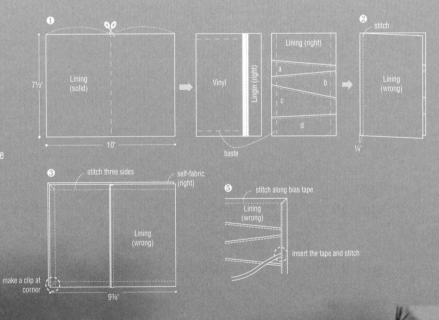

19 Romantic Ruffled Beach Skirt

Plenty of gathers in the lightweight fabric adds
a romantic feeling to this skirt.

Materials

Two pieces 25½" × 22" (65 × 56 cm) chiffon (skirt body main fabric)

Two pieces 44" × 15⅜" (112 × 39 cm) chiffon in two different print designs (ruffle main fabric)

Two pieces 24¾" × 22" (63 × 56 cm) light-colored fabric (skirt lining)

Two pieces 43" × 14" (110 × 36 cm) light-colored fabric (ruffle lining)

31½"–39½" (80–100 cm) -long drawstring (choose one with some elasticity)

Seam allowances: ¾" (2 cm) for the bottom of the ruffle and ⅜" (1 cm) for all other seam allowances

Cutting Tips

★ Cut the fabric as shown in the illustration. The skirt length is 34" (86.5 cm), but the length can be adjusted according to the wearer's height. ★ Overlock all cut edges. Use thread that matches the main fabric color.

SEWING INSTRUCTIONS

1 Fold and press a ⅜" (1 cm) waist seam allowance. Fold the seam allowance in half again and press to crease. Treat all main and lining fabrics for the skirt front and back (four panels total) in the same manner.

2 With right sides together, sew the side seams. While sewing, leave a ¾" (2 cm) hole for the drawstring at one side of the waist, as shown in the illustration. Repeat for the lining.

3 With right sides together, sew the side seams of the ruffle and press the seams open. Fold and sew the hem. Press the hem.

4 Gather the ruffle: After making two rows of running stitches at the top seam allowance, gather the fabric by pulling the threads from both ends. Gather the fabric so the ruffle's top edge is as wide as the bottom of the skirt. Distribute the gathers across the ruffle.

5 With right sides together, pin the ruffle to the bottom of the skirt. Sew along the seamline and remove the thread used for gathering the ruffle.

6 Repeat steps 1-3 for the lining.

7 Nest the lining within the main fabric and align the waistlines. Fold the hemline seam allowances of the main fabric and lining together, using the crease created in step 1 as a guide. Sew the waistline.

8 Thread the drawstring through the hole and drawstring casing. With a buttonhole stitch, sew the edges of the gap where the main fabric and lining fabric is open. Pull the drawstring to cinch the waist.

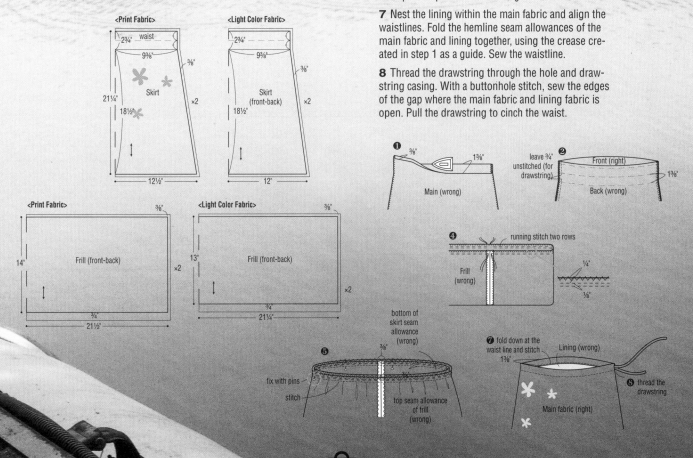

20 Sporty Mesh Skirt

This A-line skirt features slightly asymmetrical styling, inviting playful mismatched colors for the main fabric and lining.

21 Hip Sack

A key accessory for enjoying and exploring the outdoors,
a hip sack can hold small essentials while you play!

Sporty Mesh Skirt

(shown on page 80)

Materials

59" × 35½" (150 × 90 cm) mesh fabric (yellow)

59" × 35½" (150 × 90 cm) cotton lining fabric (stretch fabric in green)

Four 24" (61 cm) -long and ¾" (2 cm) -wide lengths of decorative tape

47" (120 cm) -long drawstring

Two to three appliqué numerals

Yellow thread

Seam allowances: 1¼" for the waist, ⅜" (1 cm) for the sides, and ¾" (2 cm) for the hem.

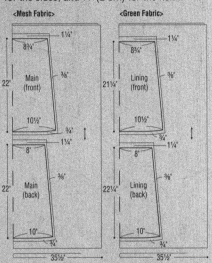

Cutting Tips

★ Cut out the sample pattern as shown in the illustration. ★ The cut edges of mesh fabric do not fray, so the edges do not need to be overlocked.

SEWING INSTRUCTIONS

1 Create the main skirt with the mesh fabric: With the right sides together, align the sides and sew the side seams. Fold and press the waist seam allowance. Press the side seams toward the center front.

2 Pin the decorative tapes the length of each side seam and sew along both edges of the tape. Sew two rows of tape to each side.

3 Fold, press, and sew the hem with yellow thread.

4 Create the lining of the skirt following steps 1–3. (Overlocking the seam allowance creates a neater look.) Press open the side seams.

5 Nest the lining within the main fabric skirt and align the waist seamlines. Fold over a 1¼" (3 cm) waist seam allowance and pin. Sew the waist seam and press.

6 Snip a hole in the center of the waist to accommodate the drawstring. (Snip only two layers fabric.) Buttonhole stitch the edges of the hole, closing the gap between one layer of main and lining fabrics. Thread the drawstring through the hole and casing with a safety pin. Knot the ends of the drawstring. Embellish the bottom edge of the skirt by affixing the appliqué numerals.

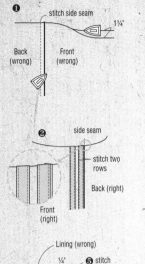

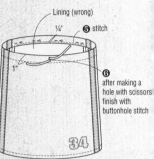

Hip Sack

(shown on page 81)

Materials

43" × 19¾" (110 × 50 cm) waterproof nylon fabric (silver)

4" × 6" (10 × 15 cm) mesh fabric (side panels)

Two 1¼" (3 cm) -wide separating zippers

One 59" (150 cm) -long piece of webbing (belt)

One pair of plastic buckles

⅝"–¾" (1.5–2 cm) -wide bias tape

Seam allowances: ⅜" (1 cm) for all seams.

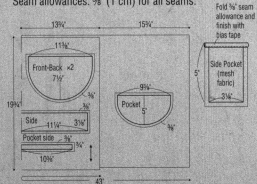

Cutting Tips

★ Cut out the sample pattern as shown in the illustration. ★ Sew bias tape to the top seam of the mesh fabric (for the pocket side panel). Sew the pocket to the position marked on the bag side panel. ★ Cut the zippers to the correct length, carefully matching the measurement of the front panel and the pocket.

SEWING INSTRUCTIONS

1 Cut the bag front and front pocket as shown. Position each zipper on the wrong side of the pocket and front pocket. Sew the zipper to each cut piece. Press.

2 With the right sides together, pin the front pocket and side panel of the pocket, matching the seams. Sew along the seam.

3 Sew the pocket to the bag front. While aligning the seamline of the bottom, determine the placement of the pocket and pin it in place. Sew them together as shown, leaving the bottom seam allowance outside.

4 With the right sides together, sew the bag front and the side panel together along the seam.

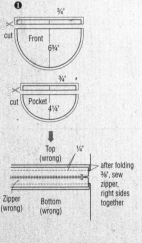

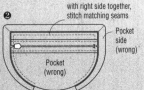

HIP SACK SEWING INSTRUCTIONS (CONT.)

5 Position the belt on the right side of bag's back panel as shown in the illustration and sew the ends.

6 With the rights sides together, and following the instructions from step 4, sew the bag's back panel and side panel together.

7 With the right sides together, lay the front and back panels flat, then fold the sides of bag in half. Sew the top seam. Turn the bag inside out through the zipper at the front panel.

8 Sew the plastic buckle to one end of the belt as shown and cut the other end to the wearer's waist measurement.

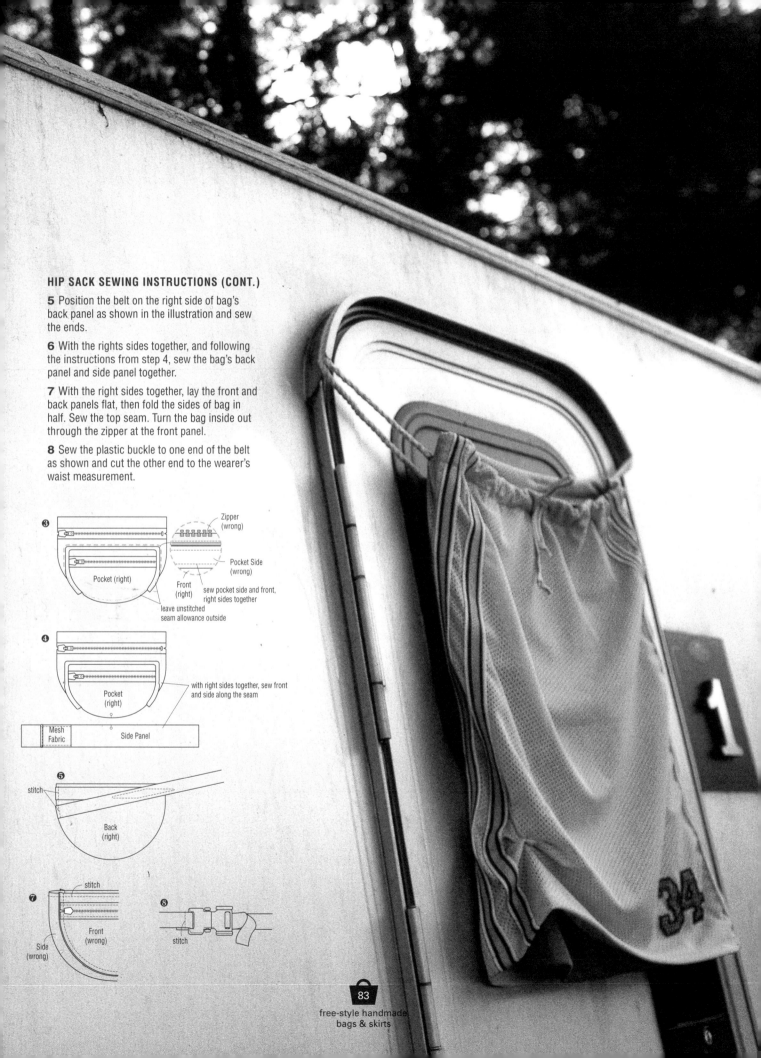

❸

Zipper (wrong)

Pocket Side (wrong)

Pocket (right)

Front (right)

sew pocket side and front, right sides together

leave unstitched seam allowance outside

❹

Pocket (right)

with right sides together, sew front and side along the seam

Mesh Fabric

Side Panel

❺

stitch

Back (right)

❼

stitch

Front (wrong)

Side (wrong)

❽

stitch

22 Compact Tote Bag

This tote bag folds into a small, coordinating zippered pouch. Pack one in your picnic bag!

Materials

35½" × 20" (90 × 51 cm) beige nylon fabric (bag body)

43" × 19¾" (110 × 50 cm) khaki fabric (this will create two bag opening pieces, two handles, two loops, and the pouch front and back)

1¼" (3 cm) -wide separating zipper

Plastic clip

¾" (2 cm) -wide bias tape

Seam allowances: ⅜" (1 cm) for all seams.

Cutting Tips

★ Cut the fabric as shown in the illustration. ★ Fold and press each ⅜" (1 cm) seam allowance for the loops. Fold each loop in half and sew along the top and bottom. Press. ★ Fold the seam allowance at both ends of the handles, then fold the handle lengthwise. Press them, then sew 1/16" (0.2 cm) away from the edge. ★ Cut the zippers to match the width of the pouch opening, adding ⅜" (1 cm) seam allowances at both ends.

SEWING INSTRUCTIONS

1 Place the khaki bag opening border piece around the bag opening. With right sides together, sew the top seam of the khaki fabric and bag body. Fold and press the seam allowance at the opposite edge of the khaki fabric. Wrap the bag opening with khaki fabric and sew the bottom edge. Topstitch the top edge.

2 With the right sides of bag front and back together, sew the side seams along the seamline. Slip plastic clip onto loop fabric. While sewing, insert the clip loop near the bag opening into the seam and continue sewing. Bind the seam allowances with bias tape.

3 Fold each corner of the bag, creating a triangular point as shown in the illustration. Sew each folded corner. Sew each handle to the inside of the bag.

4 Make the zippered pouch: Align each front piece with one side of the zipper, ¼" (0.5 cm) away from the zipper edge. Baste together and sew. (¾" (2 cm) of the zipper width will be visible.) Press.

5 With the right sides of the front and back panels together, sew the four sides. While sewing, slip one remaining loop into one pouch side seam, and sew together. Overlock all seams and turn the pouch inside out. Press the pouch to finish.

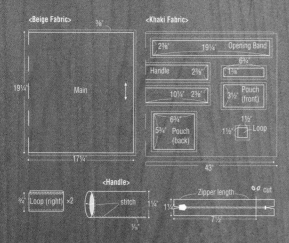

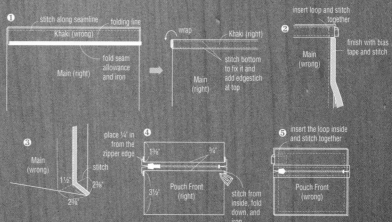

23 Apron Skirt

Wear alone as a skirt or over pants like an apron, this clever, functional skirt is a versatile addition to anyone's wardrobe.

Materials

1 yard (1 m) of 60" (150 cm) -wide coated cotton fabric

Seam allowances: 1¼" (3 cm) for the hem, and ⅜" (1 cm) for all other sides.

Cutting Tips

★ Cut out the fabric as shown in the illustration.
★ Overlock all cut edges.

SEWING INSTRUCTIONS

1 Fold the top and bottom pocket seam allowances to the wrong side. Sew the top ¼" (0.5 cm) from the edge.

2 Place the pocket panel on the skirt front's right side and baste the sides, aligning the seamline.

3 Baste the bottom pocket seam. (The pocket panel's width is larger than the skirt front.) As shown, make two ⅜" (1 cm) folds in the middle, facing outward, then sew the pocket panel into three sections. Sew the bottom of the pocket.

4 With the right sides together, align the skirt front and side panels. Sew and press the side seams.

5 Fold each seam allowance at both ends of the side panels, then sew. Fold and sew the hem. Press.

6 With the right sides together, sew the two belt pieces end to end to create a belt that is 98¼" (2.5 m) long.

7 Fold and iron the belt seam allowances. Fold the belt in half lengthwise and press.

8 With the right sides together, align the belt with the skirt top and sew along the waist seamline. Adjust the belt shape (pressing if necessary) and sew along the bottom of the belt, from one end to the other.

9 With the right sides together, sew three sides of the two pocket flap pieces, then turn the flap inside out. Topstitch the same three sides.

10 Fold a ⅜" (1 cm) seam allowance at the top of the pocket flap and sew it above the front left pocket. Fold down the flap and press. Topstitch the top edge.

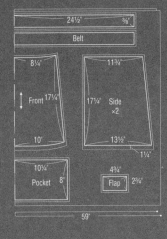

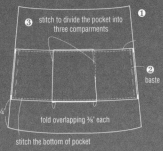

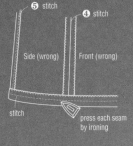

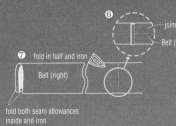

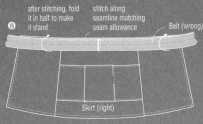

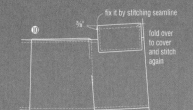

Materials

Two 9¾" × 10¾" (24.5 × 27.5 cm) pieces of rubber or vinyl fabric in sky blue (front and back)

One 3" × 19¾" (8 × 50 cm) piece of rubber or vinyl fabric in sky blue (side)

Rivets (round head preferred)

Metal rod

Awl

Wooden mallet

Plastic board

Embroidery thread and needle

Appliqués

Cutting Tips

★ Cut the pattern without leaving any seam allowances. ★ A metal rod or awl is used for making the rivet holes, and a wooden hammer and plastic board are used to set the rivets.

SEWING INSTRUCTIONS

1 Mark the placement of the rivets on the pattern with a pen. Mark the placement of the rivets on the side panel so they align with the rivets on the front and back.

2 To transfer the rivet marks, lay the pattern on top of the fabric and press the rivet marks with an awl. Repeat for the side panel.

3 Place the plastic board underneath the fabric and punch rivet holes using a metal rod and a wooden hammer.

4 Align the holes in the front and side panels. Insert a rivet and post through each hole. Hammer each rivet to secure them. Attach rivets all the way around the bag in the same manner.

5 Rubber or latex fabric tends to curl outwards when the rivets are inserted, making the bag opening widen slightly. To narrow the opening, insert additional rivets at the top of the side seam, anchoring the front and back pieces together. Alternatively, tack stitch it with embroidery thread.

6 Decorate the front of the finished bag with appliqués.

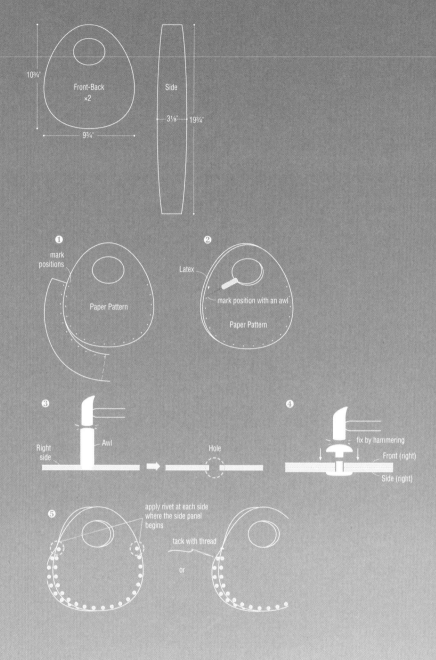

24 Round Jelly Bag

This novelty handbag is constructed with simple,
ornamental rivets—without a single stitch!

25 Denim Picnic Basket

Toting a picnic lunch has never been more fashionable with this denim carryall.

free-style handmade
bags & skirts

Denim Picnic Basket
(page 90)

Materials

One 23½" × 43" (60 × 110 cm) piece of denim fabric (bag body, bottoms, and handles)

One 19¾" × 43" (50 × 110 cm) piece of printed cotton fabric (lining and cover)

One 30" × 8" (76 × 20 cm) piece of fusible interfacing

31½" (80 cm)-long and ⅜" (1 cm)-diameter drawstring

One 10" × 6" (25 × 15 cm) piece of heavyweight paper, cardboard, or plastic (bottom insert)

Double-sided tape (or glue)

Seam allowances: 1¼" for the bag body and cover, and ⅜" (1 cm) for all other seams.

Cutting Tips

★ Fold the fabric in half and cut the fabric as shown in the illustration. ★ Round the four corners of the bottom panel. The seam allowance for the bottom should also be rounded. Make two or three ¼" (0.5 cm) -deep snips at the seam allowances of the four corners.
★ Affix the fusible interfacing to the bag body. ★ For the cover, overlock the edges after cutting the fabric.
★ For sewing with denim, change the machine sewing needle to size 14.

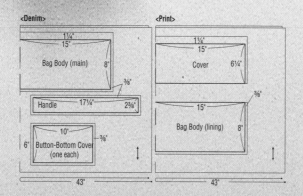

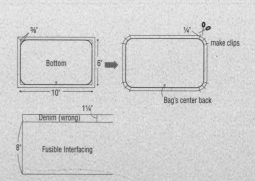

SEWING INSTRUCTIONS

1 With the right sides together, layer the lining (printed cotton) and the main fabric (denim with fusible interfacing). Pin them in place.

2 Fold the seam allowance of the opening toward the wrong side and press.

3 Sew the side seam of the body, right sides together. Press the seam open.

4 For the cover, sew each side seam, right sides together, and press the seams open. While sewing, leave ¾" (2 cm) unstitched, to accommodate the drawstring hole. Fold the seam allowance of the top and sew ⅜" (1 cm) below the edge.

5 Join the bag body and the cover. Pin the folded seam allowance (from step 2) of the bag opening and the bottom of the cover, right sides together. Sew two rows of stitching. Backtack where the side seams are joined.

6 Sew the bottom and the body of the bag. With the right sides together and beginning at the center back of the bag, align the seams of the bag's bottom and the body. Pin the bottom and body, then sew along the seamline.

7 For each handle, fold all seam allowances then fold the handle in half lengthwise. Sew a seam ⅛" (0.3 cm) away from the edge. Sew the handles to the bag opening from the inside. Turn the bag right-side out.

8 Wrap the heavyweight paper, cardboard, or plastic with denim fabric, gluing the fabric in place. Place the panel at the bottom of the bag.

9 Thread the drawstring through the hole and casing using a safety pin. Cinch the bag closed.

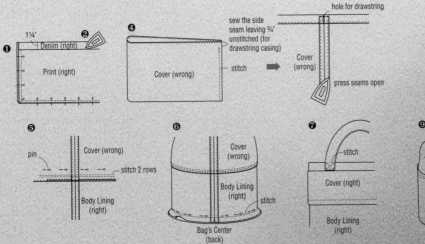

26 Patterned Flare Skirt

A voluminous skirt silhouette is constructed from six separate panels. The look and feel of the skirt varies with the scale and pattern of the fabric's print.

Materials

60" (150 cm) square printed cotton fabric

4"-6" (10-15 cm) -long zipper

Belting

Beaded trim (optional)

Seam allowances: 1½" (4 cm) for the waist, ⅜" (1 cm) for the sides, and 1¼" (3 cm) for the hem.

Cutting Tips

★ Cut six panels using the sample pattern as shown in the illustration. (Pattern layout may vary depending on the width of the fabric.) ★ If using the beaded trim, reduce the hem seam allowance to 1" (2.5 cm), so the stitched line can be hidden with the tape. ★ Overlock all cut edges.

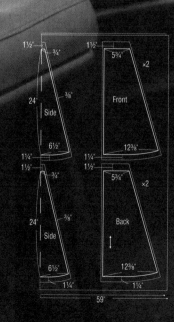

SEWING INSTRUCTIONS

1 With right sides together, sew the two front pieces and two back pieces together. Press the seams open.

2 For the two back panels, start sewing below the zipper opening.

3 Fold the right side seam allowance as shown in the illustration. For the left side seam allowance, fold ⅟₁₆" (0.2 cm) away from the seamline. Press open the seam below the zipper opening.

4 Sew the left side zipper first. Sew the right side zipper to the right side of the skirt back as shown in the illustration.

5 Join the skirt front and back to the skirt side panels.

6 Double-fold the hem—first by ⅜" (1 cm), then by ¾" (2 cm)—and pin in place. Sew the hem. (If using the beaded trim, leave a 1" hem allowance [2.5 cm] and sew as instructed, since the width of beaded tape is usually ⅝" [1.5 cm].)

7 Fold half of the waist seam allowance inside and press. Fold the waist seam allowance toward the inside again. Pin in place, then sew along the edge. Add three rows of topstitching above the seamline, reinforcing the waist. Press the skirt. If desired, sew the beaded trim along the hem.

Tips: Selecting Bag Handles

A bag's handles are second only to its fabric as design elements. Most of the bags featured here have handles made from the same fabric as the body. However, using ready-made handles can be a finishing short cut and a sure way to achieve personalized style.

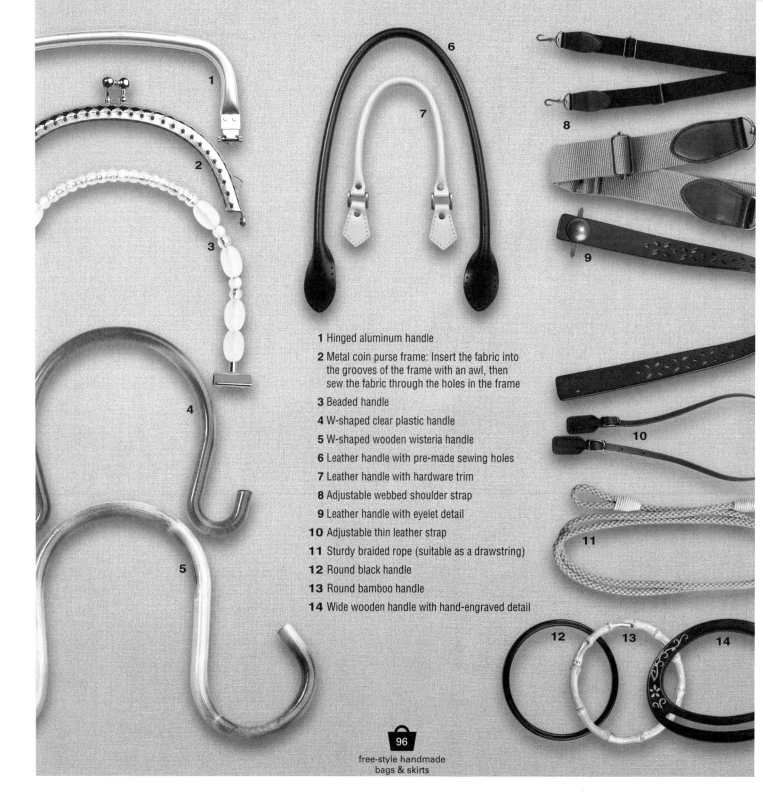

1 Hinged aluminum handle

2 Metal coin purse frame: Insert the fabric into the grooves of the frame with an awl, then sew the fabric through the holes in the frame

3 Beaded handle

4 W-shaped clear plastic handle

5 W-shaped wooden wisteria handle

6 Leather handle with pre-made sewing holes

7 Leather handle with hardware trim

8 Adjustable webbed shoulder strap

9 Leather handle with eyelet detail

10 Adjustable thin leather strap

11 Sturdy braided rope (suitable as a drawstring)

12 Round black handle

13 Round bamboo handle

14 Wide wooden handle with hand-engraved detail

Designer Profile: Hyo-Sun Jang

Hyo-Sun Jang has been a professional fashion model for ten years, working in fashions shows as well as magazines and commercials. She studied fashion design in college, and has broad knowledge of the fashion world overall. Her unique fashion sense is complemented by her keen eye for fashion trends. Her designs feature both active, practical looks and relaxed, "resort" looks. Whether designing a garment or an accessory, she demonstrates smart use of trendy fabrics, such as lightweight chiffons, mesh, and synthetic-coated fabrics.

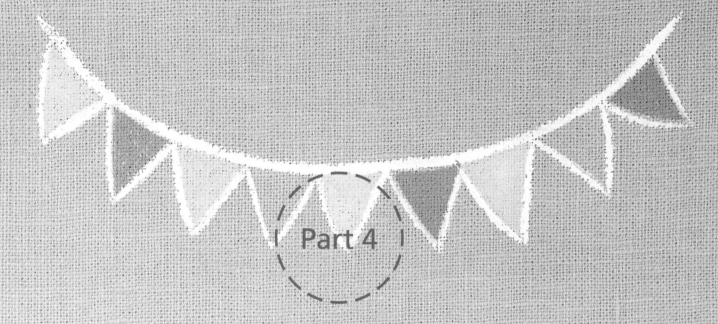

Part 4

Party

Fashionable items with unique fabric and silhouettes
are the key factors for drawing attention at a party. Wear each piece
alone or with coordinating items for special occasions.

Designs by Nam-Joo Kim

Materials

59" × 43" (150 × 110 cm) floral-print chiffon

59" × 43" (150 × 110 cm) pink lining fabric

8" (20 cm) -long invisible zipper
(to match fabric)

Fusible interfacing (for the waistband)

Seam allowances: 1¼" (3 cm) for the hem,
⅝" (1.5 cm) for the zipper opening, and ⅜"
(1 cm) for all other seams.

Cutting Tips

★ Cut the sample pattern as shown in the
illustration. ★ Overlock all cut edges. ★ Affix
the fusible interfacing on one side of the
waistband.

27 Chiffon Floral Skirt

Crinkled floral-print chiffon creates a soft,
colorful look. Pair it with a solid top
to call more attention to it.

SEWING INSTRUCTIONS

1 With right sides together, sew the side seams of the skirt front and back. Do not sew the zipper opening.

2 Gather the waist: Increase the machine's top thread tension, then sew ¼" (0.5 cm) below the waist seam. Gather the fabric by pulling the top thread only, adjusting the gathers to fit the pattern.

3 Sew the gathered waist seamline.

4 Follow steps 1-3 to create the skirt lining.

5 With right sides together, sew the top edge of two waistband pieces. Make one each for the front and back skirt. Sew the two ends together. Turn it over and press.

6 Attach the waistband: Place the front waistband against the skirt front waistline, right sides together, and pin. Sew along the waist seamline.

7 Place the back part of the waistband against the waist of the lining fabric. Sew them together from the wrong side of the fabric. Fold the seam allowances of the skirt toward the band.

8 Place the lining inside the skirt, align the waists, and sew them together right below the stitchline. Insert the zipper in the side seam (refer to page 120).

9 With right sides together, fold the belt loops in half lengthwise and sew along the bottom. Turn it inside out. Press, then edgestitch both sides. Pin each loop in place at the waistband, fold the top and bottom seam allowances inside, and sew them in place.

10 Sew the waistband ¹⁄₁₆" (0.2 cm) below the top edge from the inside.

11 Double-fold each hem of the main fabric and lining.

12 Thread a decorative ribbon through the belt loops and tie at the front.

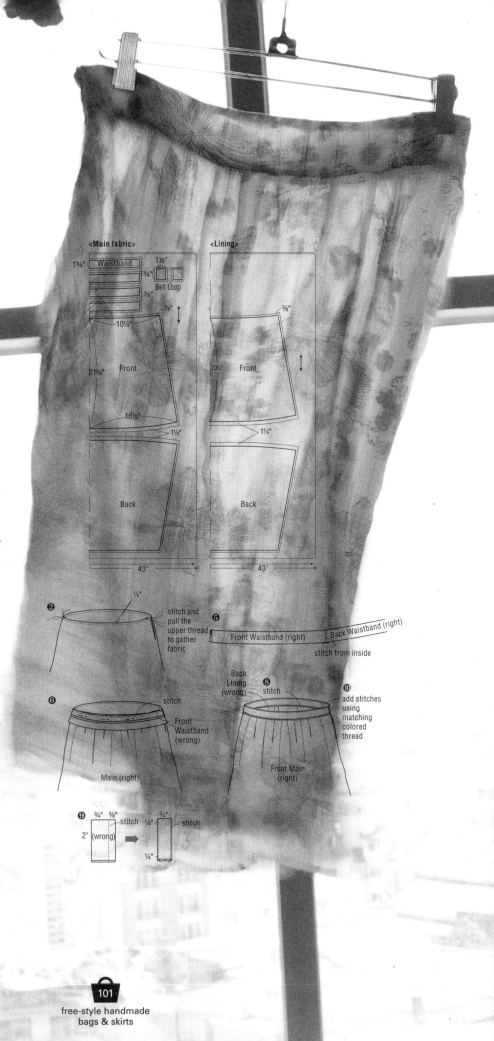

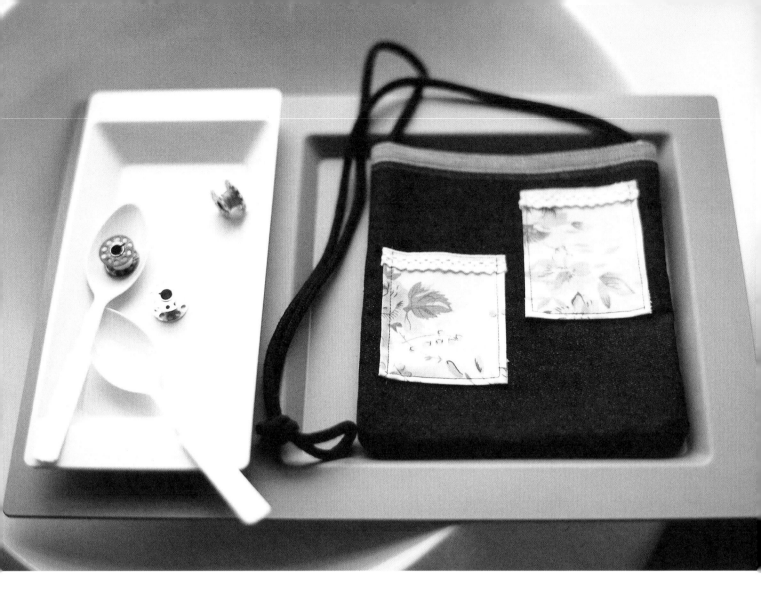

28 Pocket-Sized Shoulder Bag

A miniature shoulder bag is perfect as a party pouch. The charming patchwork appliqué is highlighted against the dark denim fabric.

Materials

Two pieces 8½" × 8¾" (21.5 × 22 cm) heavy denim

Two pieces each 2⅛" × 3⅛" (5.5 × 8 cm) and 2⅜" × 3⅛" (6 × 8 cm) fabric in different prints (patchwork)

Two pieces 3⅛" × 3½" (8 × 9 cm) fabric (pockets)

8½" (21.5 cm) -long and 1" (2.5 cm) -wide webbing

⅜" (1 cm) -wide ribbon

1½ yards (1.5 m) cord

Bias tape

Seam allowances: ⅜" (1 cm) for the sides including the bottom hem.

Cutting Tips

★ Cut the bag front, back, and patchwork fabrics as shown in the illustration. ★ Denim fabric has a tightly woven selvage. If this edge is used for the bag opening, the seam allowance does not need to be finished.

8¾"

Front-Back (denim) ×2

8½"

3⅛" Front (patch) ×2 3⅛" Front (patch) ×2

2" 2⅜"

3½" Back (patch) ×2

3⅛"

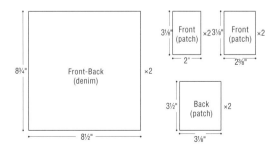

SEWING INSTRUCTIONS

1 Sew the patchwork fabrics for the bag front. Create one long strip by overlapping the fabrics' edges ¼" (0.5 cm), then sewing them.

2 Place the patchwork ¾" (2 cm) below the top edge, fold ¼" (0.5 cm) of the bottom seam allowance, then sew in place.

3 Position the webbing along the upper edge of the bag and topstitch the top and bottom.

4 Sew the lace to the upper edge of the back pockets.

5 Sew the back pockets to the back of the bag: Fold ¼" (0.5 cm) seam allowances on three sides of the pocket. Position the pockets where desired and sew them in place. Leave the bag opening unfinished.

6 With right sides together, sew the bag front and back on three sides. Finish the seam allowances with bias tape. While sewing the bias tape, insert ¾" (2 cm) of the cord within the tape and sew together. (If the fabric "sandwich" is too thick for machine sewing, hand sew it securely.)

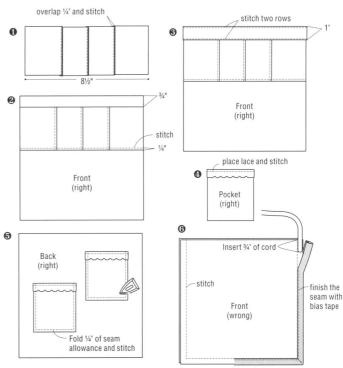

❶ overlap ¼" and stitch
8½"

❷ ¾"
stitch
¼"
Front (right)

❸ stitch two rows
1"
Front (right)

❹ place lace and stitch
Pocket (right)

❺ Back (right)
Fold ¼" of seam allowance and stitch

❻ Insert ¾" of cord
stitch
Front (wrong)
finish the seam with bias tape

29 360° Circle Skirt and Mini Handbag

Several panels of luxe fabric create creates an opulent, voluminous party skirt, paired with a cute pouch-style handbag!

Front-Back ×2   6-8" Zipper

6"
5"
4"
3"
2"
1"
0

(Brown)   (Beige)   (Pink)

b Beige   b ×4   ×4   ×4

b
1, 1"   3, 3"   5, 5"

Waist Facing

a Medium Pink
2½"
×4
4¾"
Main front-back

b Dark Pink
1¾"
4¾"   ×2
Main front-back

d Beige
8¾"
1¼"   ×2
Bag opening

c Light Pink
8¾"
Lining Front-Back
4¾"   ×2
⅝"

1¾"
×2
Main (Front-Back)

Main Lining   3¼" ×2
17¼"

104

free-style handmade
bags & skirts

Materials

1 yard (1 m) each of polyester satin in three different colors

6"-8" (15-20 cm) -long invisible zipper

Lightweight fusible interfacing

Seam allowances: ⅝" (1.5 cm) for the hem, and ⅜" (1 cm) for all other seam allowances.

Cutting Tips

★ Cut four panels of fabric for each sample pattern, except the center panel (0), of which only two are needed. (For more volume, increase number of fabric panels.)
★ The baseline waist measurement is 28¼" (72 cm), because it is a hip-hugging style.
★ The linings of full, flared skirts tend to wrap around your legs while you are walking. If the fabric is not sheer, omit the lining. However, be sure to neatly finish the seam allowances inside with overlock stitching.
★ Apply the fusible interfacing to the waist facing beforehand.

Materials

Satin fabric in four colors:

(a) 8" × 19¾" (20 × 50 cm) medium pink fabric

(b) 8" × 11¾" (20 × 30 cm) dark pink fabric

(c) 19¾" (50 cm) square light pink fabric

(d) 2" × 9⅜" (5 × 24 cm) beige fabric

19¾" (20 cm) -long white plastic separating zipper

13¾" (35 cm) -long ribbon for the strap

Two metal rings

Decorative beads

Seam allowances: ⅜" (1 cm) for all seams.

Cutting Tips

★ Using the sample pattern, cut several different kinds of fabric as shown in the illustration.
★ If using lightweight fabric, reduce the seam allowance to ¼" (0.5 cm).

SEWING INSTRUCTIONS

1 Sew four panels together to make the front of the bag and another four for the back. Sew each with right sides together and press the seams in one direction. Press from the outside and topstitch ⅛" (0.3 cm) from the seamline.

2 Fold the bag opening fabric in half and press. Place the folded edge on the right side of the zipper and sew them together. With right sides together, sew it to the front panels. Repeat for the back panel of the bag.

SEWING INSTRUCTIONS

1 With right sides together, sew panels 1-6 together. Sew each set of panels to one side of panel 0.

2 Make the skirt back as in step 1. Overlock all double-layered seams and press one side.

3 With right sides of the fabric together, sew the side seams of the skirt front and back. Leave open the left side zipper opening. Overlock the seams and press them open.

4 Insert the zipper: Align the end of the zipper to the seamline and baste in place. (Refer to page 120 for instructions on inserting a zipper.)

5 Sew one end of the waist facings together, with right sides together. Press the seam open.

6 Sew the waist facing and the skirt waistline, right sides together. Fold over the waist facing toward the inside of the skirt and press.

7 Hemstitch the ends of the facing where the zipper is set. Edgestitch the edge of waist.

8 Double-fold the hem (first by ¼" [0.5 cm], then by ⅜" [1 cm]), and sew two parallel seamlines.

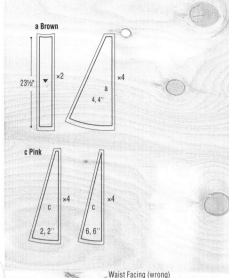

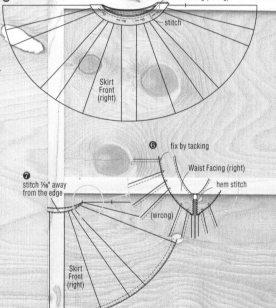

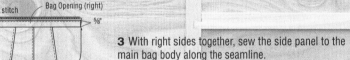

3 With right sides together, sew the side panel to the main bag body along the seamline.

4 With right sides facing, sew the front and back of the lining to the side panel lining.

5 Cut two 2⅜" (6 cm) -long pieces of ribbon. Fold the ribbon in half and place ⅝" (1.5 cm) of the folded strip at one end of the side panel, between the zipper. Slip the ribbon through one metal ring, then sew it in place. After cutting the remaining ribbon to the length desired, sew the ribbon around the metal rings.

6 Fold the opening seam allowance of the lining. Place the lining inside the bag and hemstitch by hand along the opening. While sewing, align the lining side panel to the main body by folding the sides.

7 Decorate the bag with hand-sewn beads (optional).

30 Shoulder Bag with Iron-on Transfers

This deceptively simple shoulder bag is constructed from a single panel of fabric, which is printed with an iron-on transfer you print yourself.

Materials

Two 11¾" × 21¼" (30 × 54 cm) pieces of cotton fabric in beige (bag body and lining)

Two 1½" × 2" (4 × 5 cm) pieces of fabric (loops)

Two 11" × 1¼" (28 × 3 cm) pieces of lightweight fusible interfacing

15¾" (40 cm) -long leather strap

Two 1¾" (4.5 cm) metal rings

Iron-on transfer printer paper

7½" × 3⅞" (19 × 10 cm) piece of thick paper (or plastic sheet)

Seam allowances: ⅜" (1 cm) for four sides of the bag.

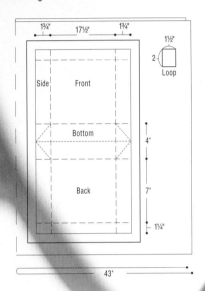

Cutting Tips

★ Cut the fabric as shown in the illustration.
★ Overlock all cut edges. ★ Affix the fusible interfacing to the top and bottom of the bag: Align interfacing 1¼" (3 cm) from the edges, cover with thin fabric, and press. ★ With an inkjet printer, print the bag design(s) on sheets of iron-on transfer paper (one sheet of iron-on transfer paper for each side of the bag.) Place the transfer paper on the fabric face down and press. (Use only 100% cotton or polyester fabric for the bag, and avoid coated fabrics, wool, and silk.) ★ Create the ring loops: Fold a ⅜" (1 cm) seam allowance from both sides of the 1½" (4 cm) -wide fabric, and sew ¼" (0.5 cm) from the edges.

SEWING INSTRUCTIONS

1 Fold the seam allowance of the bag opening and press lightly. Fold again at the bottom of the fusible interfacing and sew along the edge. Repeat on the opposite end.

2 With right sides together, fold the entire bag in half. Pin the side seams in place and sew them. Press all the seams in one direction.

3 Fold each corner of the bag, creating a triangular point. Sew a diagonal line across the corner. Trim the triangle ⅜" (1 cm) from the seam. Overlock the cut edges, or fold them to the bottom and hand-sew the edges.

4 Sew the lining in the same manner as the bag body. Leave a 1½–2" (4–5 cm) -long gap in one side seam (for turning the bag inside out in step 7).

5 Turn the right side of the bag body to the outside and nest it within the bag lining.

6 Slip the metal rings into the ring loops. Center the loops on the sides, placing the bottom edges of the loops ⅜" (1 cm) between the bag body and lining. Align the bag opening seamlines and sew around the opening, sewing through the metal ring loops, too.

7 Pull the bag body through the hole in the lining, turning the entire bag inside out. Hemstitch to complete the seam.

8 To reinforce the loops, sew them again with thread that matches the color of the fabric.

9 Thread the leather strap through the metal rings and hand sew the ends securely. (If the leather strap does not have premade holes for sewing, create them with an awl.)

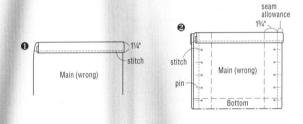

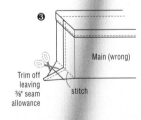

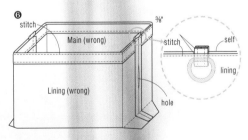

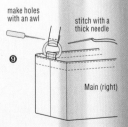

31 Reversible Tote

This gold and black reversible bag has a sophisticated, modern design. Each side features unique design details.

Reversible Tote
(shown on page 108)

Materials

Two pieces 12⅝" × 30" (32 × 76 cm) fabric: one gold (main fabric) and one black (lining)

Two 11¾" (30 cm) -long strips 1¼"–1⅜" (3–3.5 cm) -wide webbing

Ribbon

19¾" (50 cm) -long buckled leather handle

Seam allowances: ⅜" (1 cm) for all seams.

SEWING INSTRUCTIONS

1 Sew each end of the decorative leather handle to the front and back of the bag. (Separate the buckle before sewing, attaching each side at its desired position.)

2 With right sides together, fold the main fabric in half and sew the side seams.

3 Fold each corner of the bag, creating triangular points. Sew a line across the corner. Trim the triangle ⅜" (1 cm) from the seam. Overlock the cut edges, or fold them to the bottom and hand-sew the edges.

4 Sew the lining in the same manner as the bag body.

5 Turn the bag body inside out, so the right side faces outside. Edgestitch all folded edges ¹⁄₁₆" (0.2 cm) from all sides. Repeat for the lining.

6 With right sides together, align the bag openings of the main fabric and lining. Insert the handles between the two layers of fabric. Pin along the bag openings and sew. Leave a 4" (10 cm) -wide hole at one side.

7 Pull the bag body through the hole, turning the bag inside out. Tuck in the seam allowance of the hole and pin. Topstitch two rows at the bag opening.

8 Finish the bag by tucking in the lining. Optional: decorate the bag with a corsage sewn from several ribbons.

Fitted Skirt with Back Slit
(shown on page 111)

Materials

1 yard of 43" (110 cm) -wide cotton or polyester blend fabric

6" (15 cm) invisible zipper

Large hook and bar

Belting

Seam allowances: ¾" (2 cm) for the hem, and ⅜" (1 cm) for all other seams.

Cutting Tips

★ Cut the fabric as shown in the illustration. ★ Overlock all cut edges. ★ Fold the darts in the skirt back in half, pin them in place, then sew the darts. Backtack both ends of the dart seamlines. Press the darts toward the center back. ★ Place the belting at the wrong side of front waistband and secure them with pins.

SEWING INSTRUCTIONS

1 Join the skirt front and side panels: With right sides together, sew both side panels to the center panel. Press the seams toward the center front. Topstitch ¹⁄₁₆" (0.2 cm) from both seamlines.

2 Join the back panels: With right sides together, sew the two back panels, except for the zipper opening and the slit. Backtack both ends of the seamlines.

3 Insert the zipper at the back (refer to page 120 for how to insert a zipper).

4 Create the slit. Fold the seam allowances for the slit from the edges of both panels. Fold the left side, matching the seamline to the center back, and press. Sew a diagonal line from inside where the slit ends. Finish the slit by adding a stitch to the folded edge (as shown in the illustration).

5 With right sides together, sew the side seams of the finished skirt front and skirt back. Press the side seams open.

6 Double-fold the hem ⅜" (1 cm) and stitch.

7 With right sides together, sew the two pieces of the waistband together. Turn the waistband inside out and press.

8 Refer to steps 9–11 of Making a Basic Skirt (see page 22) and sew the waistband to the skirt.

9 Fold the seam allowance of the waistband facing and pin it. Secure the waistband by sewing ¹⁄₁₆" (0.2 cm) above the seamline. Topstitch the other three sides.

10 Attach the hook and bar above the zipper (see page 120).

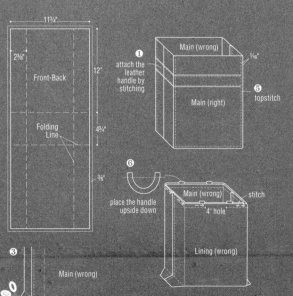

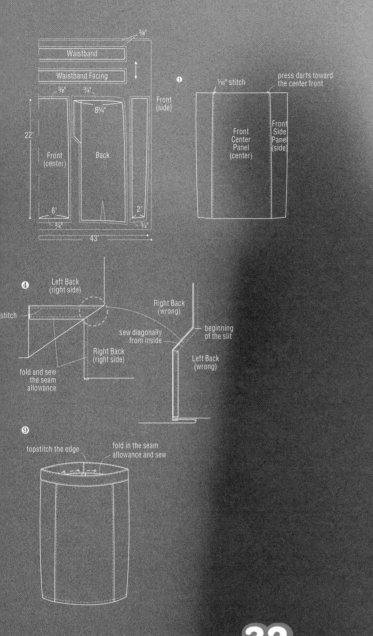

Waistband

Waistband Facing

⅜"

❶

Front
(side)

½" stitch

press darts toward
the center front

⅜" ¾"

8¾"

22"

Front
(center)

Back

Front
Center
Panel
(center)

Front
Side
Panel
(side)

6"

2"

¾"

¾"

43"

❹

Left Back
(right side)

stitch

Right Back
(wrong)

sew diagonally
from inside

beginning
of the slit

Right Back
(right side)

Left Back
(wrong)

fold and sew
the seam
allowance

❾

topstitch the edge

fold in the seam
allowance and sew

32 Fitted Skirt with Back Slit

This basic skirt is just as suitable for a formal party as it is for everyday occasions. It is unlined and made of light, summer-weight fabric with a slit at the back, allowing for ease of movement.

111

free-style handmade
bags & skirts

free-style handmade
bags & skirts

33 Polka-Dot Tiered Skirt

The natural shirring of each tier creates a light silhouette for these matching, "mother-daughter" skirts.

Pink Polka-Dot Three-Tiered Skirt
(shown on page 112)

Materials

2 yards 59" (150 cm) -wide polka-dot chiffon

2 yards 43" (110 cm) -wide polyester fabric in pink

6"–8" (15–20 cm) -long invisible zipper

27½" (70 cm) -long ribbon

Lightweight fusible interfacing

Seam allowances: ½" (0.8 cm) for the hem, and ⅜" (1 cm) for all other seams.

Cutting Tips

★ Cut the fabric as shown in the illustration. Select a chiffon fabric that does not stretch along or against the grainline. ★ Only sharp scissors should be used to cut thin, delicate fabrics such as chiffon. ★ Apply the fusible interfacing inside the waist facing.

<Polka-Dot Fabric>   59"
a Front   b Front
21¼"   23"
Zipper
⅜"
a Back   b Back
⅜"

<Pink Fabric>
Waist Facing
c Front   24⅜"
c Back
43"

Variation A:
Pink Polka-Dot Three-Tiered Skirt
(shown on page 112)

SEWING INSTRUCTIONS

1 Sew each skirt front panel to each back panel (a, b, and c). With right sides together, sew each side seam, leaving an opening for the zipper.

2 Overlock the side seam allowances.

3 Fold and press ⅛" (0.3 cm) of the skirt hem. Fold ¼" (0.5 cm) again and sew the hem.

4 Align the three layers at the waistline, longest layer on the inside. Pin along the waist. Sew ¼" (0.5 cm) below the waistline.

5 Place the right side of the waist facing the skirt's right side. Baste the waist seamline, then sew. Turn up the waist facing and fold it inside the skirt. Fold in the seam allowances at both ends (where the zipper will be inserted). Press.

6 Sew the ribbon trim around the waist. Secure the ribbon with double-sided tape and sew two seamlines, each ¹⁄₁₆" (0.2 cm) from top and bottom.

7 Insert the zipper (refer to page 120 for how to insert a zipper). (Insert the zipper between the skirt and the waist facing.)

8 Hemstitch the bottom of the waist facing's seam allowance and the inner skirt.

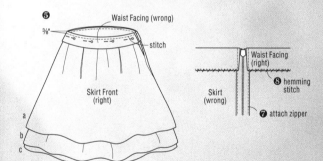

Variation B:
Girls' Skirt with Elastic Waistband
(shown on page 113)

Materials

2 yards (2 m) 59" (150 cm) -wide polka-dot chiffon

One 14" × 4" (36 × 10 cm) piece of stretch fabric

20" (50 cm) -long drawstring

Seam allowances: ½" (0.8 cm) for the hem, and ⅜" (1 cm) for all other seams.

Cutting Tips

★ Cut the fabric as shown in the illustration.

SEWING INSTRUCTIONS

1 Gather the waist of each tier: Sew ¼" (0.5 cm) below the waist seamline with a long, loose machine stitch. Pull the upper thread to gather, matching each tier's width to the waist circumference.

2 Sew the side seams of each panel (a, b, and c). Overlock the layered seam allowances.

3 Follow the tier hemming instructions for Variation A.

4 Align the three layers at the waistline, longest layer on the inside. Pin along the waist. Sew ⅛" (0.3 cm) below the seam allowance.

5 Snip two holes in the center of the band for the drawstring. Finish the holes' edges with a buttonhole stitch.

6 With right sides together, sew the ends. Turn it inside out and fold in half. Press the band.

7 Insert the band (folded edge facing down) at the waist of the skirt's right side, pin, and sew all the way around. Finish the seam allowances by overlocking them together. Turn up the band and press. Thread the drawstring through the hole.

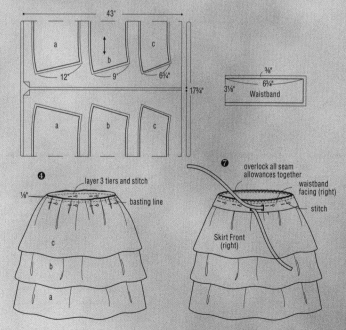

34 Asian-Style Bag

A modern floral-patterned fabric and wooden
handles combine in this fusion-style handbag.

Asian-Style Bag
(shown on page 116)

Materials

½ yard (50 cm) 43" (110 cm) -wide printed heavy cotton fabric (bag body)

½ yard (50 cm) 43" (110 cm) -wide solid heavy cotton fabric (lining)

Two W-shaped wooden handles

Six buttons

One snap

Lightweight fusible interfacing

Seam allowances: ⅜" (1 cm) for all seams.

Cutting Tips

★ Cut the fabric as shown in the illustration. ★ Affix the fusible interfacing to the wrong side of each fabric. ★ Snip ⅛"–¼" (0.3–0.5 cm) -long clips at marked notches. ★ Sew ⅝" (1.5 cm) -wide and 3" (8 cm) -long loops for the handles.

SEWING INSTRUCTIONS

1 To make pleats, fold the darts matching the marks in the pattern—as though folding skirt darts—and sew the top edge.

2 Sew the front and back panel to the side panel. With right sides together, align the curved seamlines and pin them. Sew the curved corners, gently pulling the thread to create shirring. Sew along the seamline. Press the seam open.

3 Topstitch the side panel along the seamlines.

4 Create a pouch for the lining (as instructed in step 2).

5 With right sides together, sew the bag opening and its facing, but stop sewing ⅜" (1 cm) from the bottom edge. While sewing, insert the loops for the handles and sew together. Trim the seam allowances of the loops, leaving ⅛" (0.3 cm) inside.

6 Turn inside out and press.

7 Face the front side and bag front's right side together and sew.

8 Nest the lining inside the bag and sew the lining and facing of the bag opening. Align the folded seam allowance of the lining and the opening facing's seamline. Sew as shown in the illustration.

9 Bring the front and back opening together and sew both sides ⅛" (0.3 cm) from the edges. Edgestitch the top.

10 Attach the decorative buttons to the front and back. Sew the snaps to the inside the bag. Slip the handles into the loops.

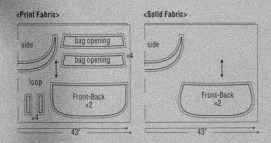

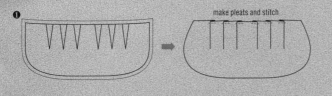

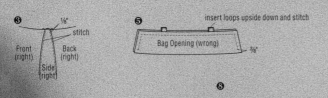

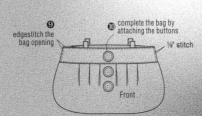

35 Casual Panel Skirt

This asymmetrical design has a decorative, pleated fabric panel grafted to the front of the skirt.

Casual Panel Skirt

Materials

1 yard (1 m) of 59" (150 cm) -wide khaki fabric

1 yard (1 m) of striped fabric

Five buttons

Fusible interfacing

Seam allowances: For khaki fabric, ¾" (2 cm) for
the hem, 1" (2.5 cm) for the sides for skirt front,
and ⅜" (1 cm) for all other seams. For striped fabric,
⅝" (1.5 cm) for the hem, ¼" (0.5 cm) for the sides,
and ⅜" (1 cm) for all other seams.

Cutting Tips

★ Cut the fabric as shown in the illustration.
★ Apply the fusible interfacing to the waistband.

SEWING INSTRUCTIONS

1 Pin and sew all darts in the khaki and striped fabrics. Backtack the beginning and end of the stitch.
Press the seams toward the center. Fold a ¼" (0.5 cm)
seam allowance in the skirt front, then fold in ¾"
(2 cm) again. Sew two rows at the top and bottom
of the folded seam allowance.

2 With right sides together, sew the skirt front
to the skirt back. Press the seams open.

3 Fold the hem ¼" (0.5 cm) and press. Fold the
hem ⅝" (1.5 cm), pin, and sew.

4 Pleat the bottom panels of the skirt front and back
of the decorative fabric. On the front bottom panel,
starting 2½" (6.5 cm) from one side, make 1" (2.5 cm)
-wide pleats and press them. To secure the pleats, add
¹⁄₁₆" (0.1 cm) -wide stitches inside the pleats. Sew each
pleat 6" (15 cm) from the top edge.

5 Sew the decorative panel to the upper panels.
Topstitch the seamline. Double-fold the hem and sew.

6 Place the pleated panel against the khaki skirt.
Pin the sides and waistline. Sew the folded side edges
to the skirt.

7 Sew the waistband with right sides together, then
turn it inside out. Press. With right sides together, sew
the waistband front to the skirt. Fold in and press the
seam allowance of the waistband facing.

8 Sew the waist and topstitch all sides of waistband.

9 Snip buttonholes at the marked positions and attach
the buttons. Sew four belt loops around the waistband.

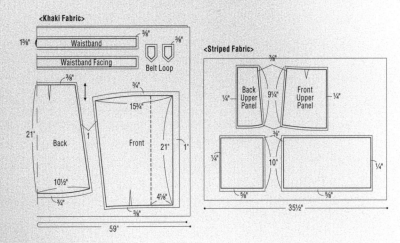

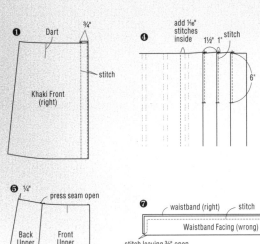

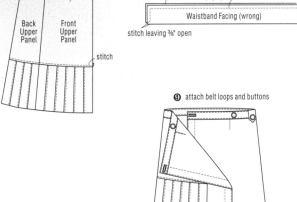

Tips: Finishing Details

INSERTING A ZIPPER

Different styles of zippers are inserted in different ways. In this book, most zippers are inserted at the waists of skirts. For a front or side zipper in a skirt, the wearer's left side will have a zipper flap; for a back zipper in the skirt, it is the opposite. The sample zipper length used here is 6" (15 cm) long. To attach a front or a side zipper:

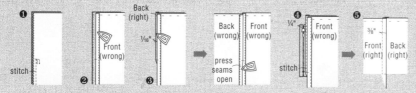

1 With right sides together, sew just below the zipper opening at the side seam. Baste the zipper opening.
2 Press the seam allowance of the front panel along the seamline.
3 For the seam allowance of the back panel, fold 1/16" (0.2 cm) from the seamline. Press open the seams below the zipper opening.
4 Begin to sew the zipper at the skirt back (as shown).
5 Turn the skirt inside out so the right side faces out. Place the zipper at the wrong side of the skirt front, and sew the zipper as shown. Remove the basting thread.

ATTACHING SNAPS

Using a needle and thread, first attach the ball half of the snap. Make an impression on the facing fabric to mark the placement for the socket half. Sew the socket half.

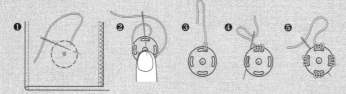

1 Knot the thread through the snap as shown.
2 Starting from the right side of a hole, insert the needle from the underside and pull it through the hole. Wrap the thread around the needle and insert the needle again, creating a basic buttonhole stitch. Sew through only one layer of fabric to make it invisible from the reverse side.
3 Cinch the knot. Repeat the stitch three or four times in each hole.
4 Repeat the buttonhole stitch in all holes.
5 Insert the needle through one layer of fabric and pull it out at the other end. Create a knot, pull the thread underneath the snap, and snip it.

ATTACHING A HOOK AND BAR

A hook and bar is attached to a waistband above a zipper as a closure. The buttonhole stitch is also used.

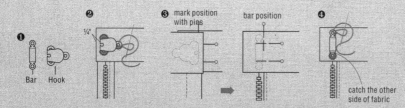

1 The hook is sewn to the overlap and the bar to the underlap.
2 Buttonhole stitch the hook 1/4" (0.5 cm) in from the edge. (Sew though only the fusible interfacing so the stitch does not show from the reverse side.)
3 Mark the position for the bar with pins as shown.
4 Buttonhole stitch the bar in place.

Nam-Joo Kim graduated from ESMOD Seoul. Currently a women's apparel designer at Basic House, Kim has a savvy eye for capturing the latest fashion trends. Within this chaper, she presents a range of individual styles, including formal, romantic, casual, and cute. Her designs often feature coordinating items that use matching fabrics and colors.

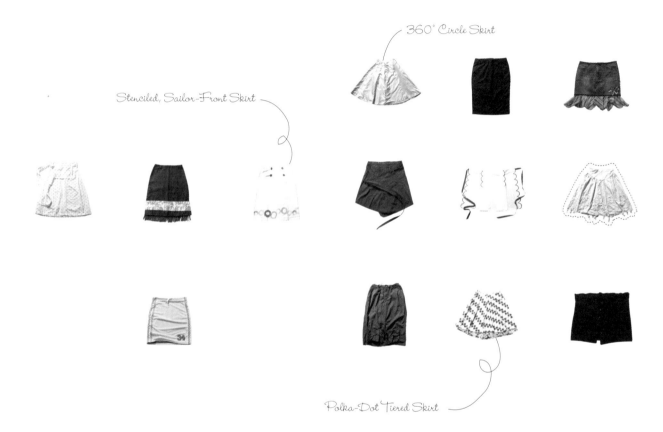

360° Circle Skirt

Stenciled, Sailor-Front Skirt

Polka-Dot Tiered Skirt

Chiffon Floral Skirt

Vintage-Style Long Skirt With Pockets

choose your favorite!

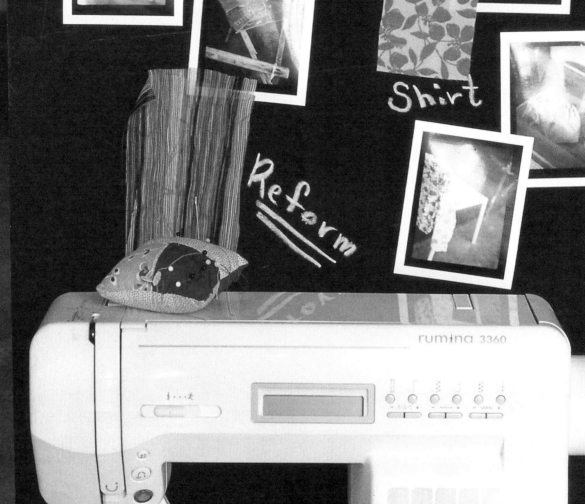

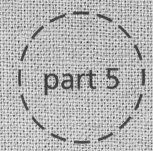

part 5

Reform + Remake

Cut up, refashion, and sew gently used tops and bottoms for 100% new ideas!

Designs by Minimili

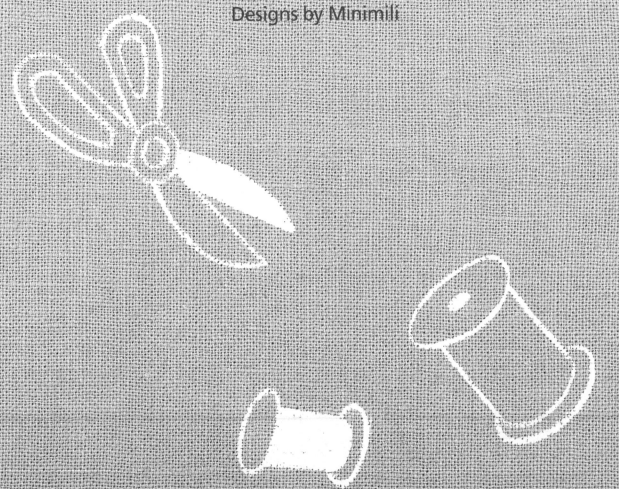

Materials

Knee-length denim skirt

Short-sleeved lightweight chiffon blouse

1½ yards (1.5 m) of ⅜" (1 cm) -wide lace

19¾" (50 cm) -long sequin trim

Small hook and eye

36 Vintage-Style Miniskirt

Slice an out-of-date, knee-length denim skirt and refashion it into a cute miniskirt. Chiffon ruffles salvaged from a lightweight blouse decorate the hem of the skirt.

Cutting Tips

★ Remove the waistband from the skirt with fabric scissors. Remove the belt loops and tags. ★ Cut the skirt so it falls 6" (15 cm) above the knee. Overlock the cut edge of the skirt. ★ Remove the ruffled sleeves from the blouse with fabric scissors. The width of the ruffle should be about 4" (10 cm).

SEWING INSTRUCTIONS

1 Sew the hook and eye to the skirt above the zipper.

2 Position the ruffle along the skirt hem: Overlap the skirt hem with the ruffle by about ¼" (0.5 cm), baste ruffle in place, and sew along the hem. Place the lace along the stitch line and sew the top and bottom edges.

3 For added flair, create a freestyle pattern using sequin trim, beaded details, or other embellishments.

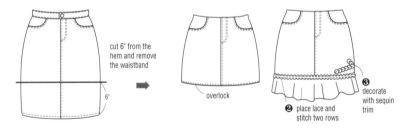

cut 6" from the hem and remove the waistband

6"

overlock

❷ place lace and stitch two rows

❸ decorate with sequin trim

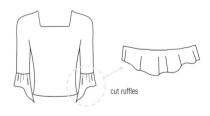

cut ruffles

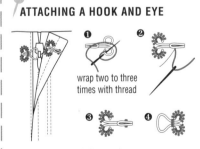

ATTACHING A HOOK AND EYE

❶ ❷

wrap two to three times with thread

❸ ❹

Buttonhole stitch is used to attach a hook and eye.

SEWING A SEQUIN TRIM

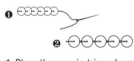

❶

❷

1 Place the sequin trim where desired. With a needle and thread, pass the needle through the fabric and make a knot at the back.

2 Sew between every one or two sequins to secure the trim.

37 Drawstring-Waist Skirt

This skirt is crafted from a pair of track pants and features an adjustable back slit. The width of the skirt can be adjusted using draping techniques.

Materials

One pair of cotton pants with drawstring waist

Cutting Tips

★ Rip open the inseam of the pants from the bottom to the end of zipper.

SEWING INSTRUCTIONS

1 For the skirt front, determine the skirt width, pin the skirt, and sew.

2 Sew the skirt back: Depending on the skirt's desired width, overlap the two pant legs and pin them. Sew along the former seamline. (As the the skirt width widens, the back slit will get deeper.)

3 Cut the skirt to the length desired.

4 From the trimmed fabric, create 4"–6" (10–15 cm) -wide strips and sew them to the skirt front. Sew two rows of running stitches at the center of the strip lengthwise and pull the thread to gather until the strip is the same width as the front skirt. Sew it to the skirt. Remove the running stitch thread.

5 Leave the top and bottom edges of the decorative strip and the skirt hem raw.

rip inner seams

① with right sides together stitch from wrong side

③ cut the length as you desire

② beginning of ripped seam

stitch along previously stitched line

④ pull from both sides

make holes to decorate

two rows of running stitch

skirt front width

stitch

38 Camouflage Straight Skirt

This classic reform + remake design combines a strong
statement with simple straight lines.

39 Oversized Camouflage Tote

Crafted from a military jacket, this bag has an authentic feel.
This pattern can be adapted to a number of tote bags in various sizes.

Camouflage Straight Skirt
(shown on page 130)

Materials

One pair of military pants

One button and a shoulder strap from a military jacket

Cutting Tips

★ Remove the inside seams of the military pants. Try on the pants and close the button at the waist. The bottom is divided into two panels. ★ Cut the legs to the desired length, including a 1½" (4 cm) seam allowances for the skirt hem. ★ Remove any unwanted exterior pockets (optional) ★ Refer to draping instructions on page 142.

SEWING INSTRUCTIONS

1 Sew the front and back of the skirt along the pinned line. Leave the existing (ripped) seams folded and sew two rows along the previous stitched line.

2 Turn the skirt inside out. Overlock the seam allowance and trim the excess fabric.

3 Fold hem ⅜" (1 cm) and press. Fold hem 1¼" (3 cm) again and pin. Sew along the fold and press.

4 Adorn the waist with a military-style shoulder strap and button.

remove the pocket

rip inseam

cut the legs including the seam allowance

If the waist is bigger than your size, rip the seam and stitch again

❶

Back (right)

stitch two rows

trim off excess fabric after overlocking the seam allowance

❷

Back (wrong)

❹

decorative button

adorn the waist with a shoulder strap from the jacket

Oversized Camouflage Tote
(shown on page131)

Materials

One military jacket

Small piece of black denim fabric

Military pattern mesh fabric (lining)

Fusible interfacing

1½" (4 cm) -wide webbing

Two snaps

One plastic mesh sheet

¾" (2 cm) -wide bias tape

Seam allowances: 1¼" for the bag opening, and ⅜" (1 cm) for all other seams.

Cutting Tips

★ Cut the military jacket as shown in the illustration. ★ Include the curved armholes to incorporate the jacket pockets. Fill in the curved armhole with patches of black denim. ★ Use the jacket sleeves for the side and bottom panel of the bag. Cut rectangular shapes that match the measurements of the front and back of the bag. ★ Cut the fusible interfacing to match the seamline of each panel (except the bottom). ★ Cut the lining fabric to the same size as the main fabric. ★ Bag measurements vary depending on the size of the jacket you are using.

SEWING INSTRUCTIONS

1 Sew patches to the armholes to complete the rectangular shapes.

2 Affix the fusible interfacing to the wrong side of the front, back, and sides of the bag.

3 Pin the lining pieces to each panel of the main bag fabric inside the seamline.

4 With right sides together, sew the front and side panels. Repeat for the back panel.

5 Place all side panels against the bottom of the bag, pin together, and sew one side at a time. Finish the seam allowances with bias tape.

6 Fold and press half of the bag opening's seam allowance. Fold it again and sew around the opening. Finish the seam allowances with bias tape.

7 Pin the handles in place and sew along the edges. Do not sew the pockets.

8 Wrap the plastic mesh with lining fabric and place it at the bottom of the bag.

9 Attach the snaps to the inside side panels.

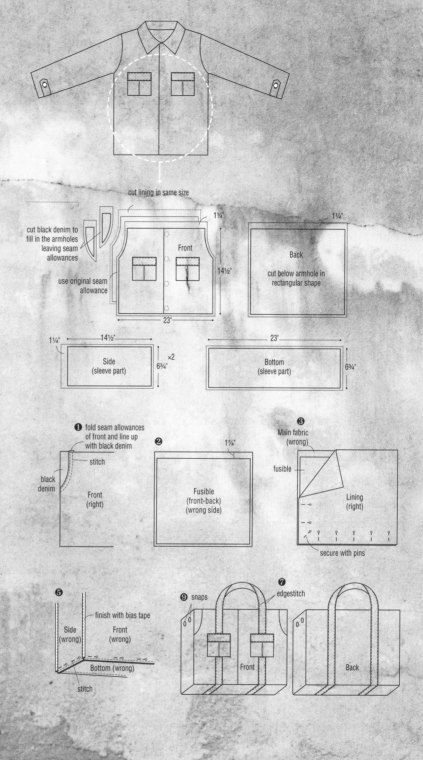

40 Reversible Denim Bag

This reversible leather-handled bag features one side that has a neat, finished look and another with frayed edges.

Materials

1 pair of jeans

1 yard (1 m) of 45" (115 cm) -wide floral-printed fabric

Fusible interfacing

Leather handles and matching embroidery thread

Seam allowance (main fabric): 1½" (4 cm) for the bag opening

Cutting Tips

★ Cut the legs from the jeans and spread them flat on the work surface. Press them and trim them into a rectangle. Cut the denim to the dimensions shown in the illustration. ★ Cut the floral-printed fabric to the same dimensions as the denim plus a 1½" (4 cm) seam allowance for the bag opening. ★ Cut the fusible interfacing to the same dimensions as the denim without leaving any seam allowances.

SEWING INSTRUCTIONS

1 With right-sides together, pin the bag pieces together along the seam edges.

2 Keeping right sides together, sew the bag front to the sides with a ⅜"(1 cm) seam allowance. Fold the side panels at the corners. Snip the corners from the inside bottom seams.

3 Sew the bag back to the sides as instructed in step 2.

4 Double-fold the top hem so it measures ¾" (2 cm) and press. Pin the hem in place and turn the bag inside out. Sew the hem.

5 Place the handles where desired and hand sew them to the bag.

13¾" Lining Front-Back (denim) ×2

11¾"

1½"

13¾" Main fabric Front-Back (print fabric) ×2

11¾"

39¼"

Lining Side (Print)

4¾"

39¼"

Self-side (denim)

4¾"

1½"

1½"

❶

Main fabric (wrong)

fusible

Lining (right)

fix with pins

❷

Side

⅜"

stitch

Front (lining)

make clips

❹

13¼"

Main (right)

fold the opening and stitch

4"

11"

41 Vintage-Style Handbag

A vintage shift dress is re-formed into a square bag.
The side darts at the bag front naturally create volume
in the front.

Materials

One sleeveless dress

¼" (0.5 cm) -diameter wooden dowels (for the handles)

Seam allowance: ¾" (2 cm) for the bottom

Cutting Tips

★ Cut the dress bodice into the size desired. Select a dress made of heavy, non-stretch fabric. ★ If necessary, trim to align the front and back sides. If the back panel has a zipper, remove it and sew the overlapping fabric to close the gap. ★ Use trimmed fabric to wrap the wooden handles and bind the necklines.

SEWING INSTRUCTIONS

1 Rip open both shoulder seams.

2 Turn inside out and sew the bottom edges closed.

3 Cut the neck facing fabric. Leave about ½" (0.7 cm) seam allowance at the top and bottom. Place it at the right side of the back neck and pin them along the seamline.

4 Snip facing fabric ¼" (0.5 cm) deep around the top and bottom edges.

5 With right sides facing, fold over the seam allowance toward the wrong side of the back. Sew seam, then fold over the entire facing and press. Make snips at the bottom seam allowance as well, fold it inside, and sew.

6 Wrap the handles with the remaining fabric.

7 For the handle casing, fold in ¼" (0.5 cm) and press.

8 Insert the handle, wrap the handle, and sew it from the inside.

9 Hemstitch the sides using matching color thread. Tack stitch below the handles to secure them.

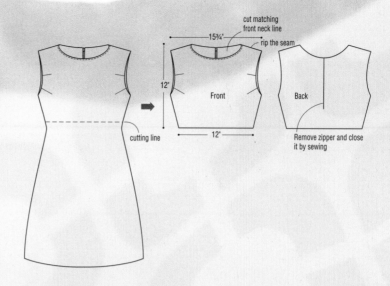

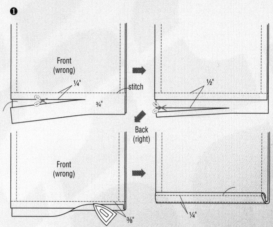

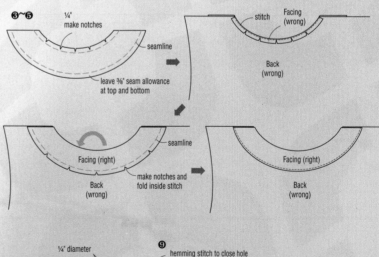

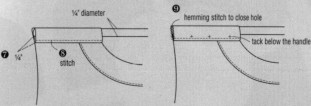

42 Layered Knit Wrap

This modified cardigan can be tied around your waist as a light layer over both pants and skirts.

Materials

Knit cardigan

A hook and bar

Cutting Tips

★ Cut a straight line across the front and back of the cardigan below the armhole. ★ Create waist ties with the leftover fabric. ★ Use a ball-point machine needle (size 9 or 10) and elastic thread for sewing with knit fabrics.

SEWING INSTRUCTIONS

1 Fold the cut edges ⅜" (1 cm) and sew along the edge.

2 Leave seam allowances as long as the front panel on each of the two waist ties.

3 Sew ⅜" (1 cm) from the inside at the sides where the ties begin. Wrap the top edge of the front panel with the seam allowance and sew along the edge.

4 Topstitch all sides of the waist ties.

5 If the original cardigan's first button is not positioned at the top edge, attach the hook and bar (see page 120).

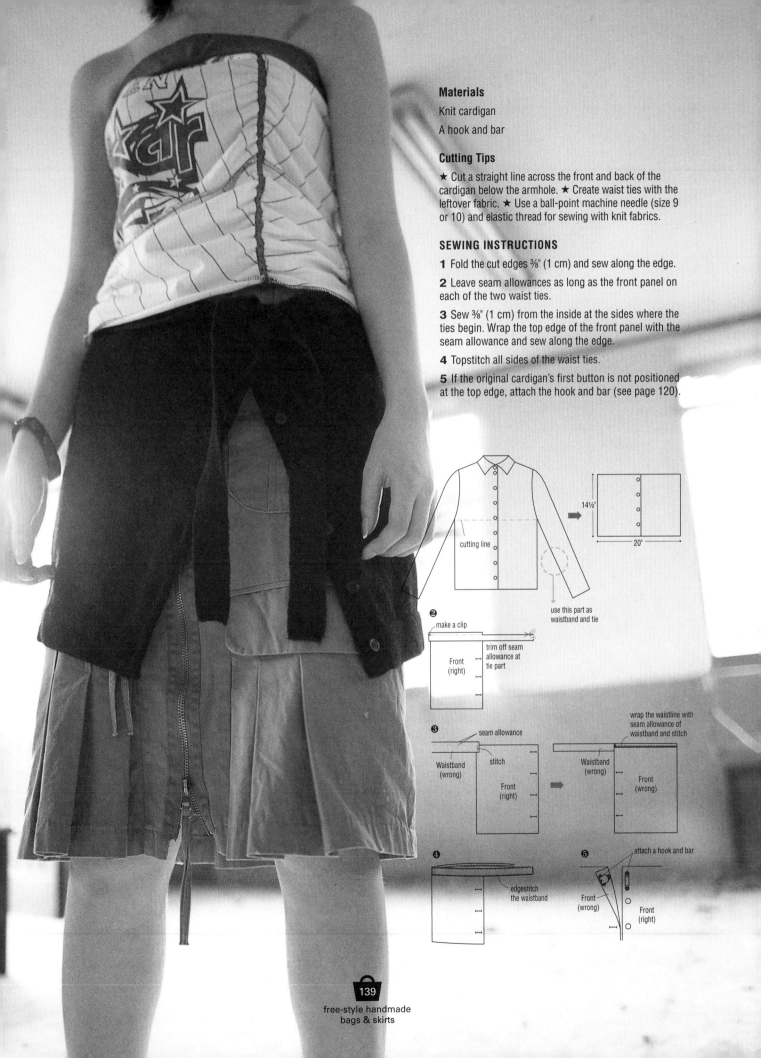

cutting line

14½"

20"

use this part as waistband and tie

❷ make a clip

trim off seam allowance at tie part

Front (right)

❸ seam allowance

stitch

Waistband (wrong)

Front (right)

wrap the waistline with seam allowance of waistband and stitch

Waistband (wrong)

Front (wrong)

❹ edgestitch the waistband

❺ attach a hook and bar

Front (wrong)

Front (right)

43 Nostalgic Messenger Bag

This vintage-style shoulder bag is crafted from a dated, printed tablecloth.

Materials

Tablecloth

1 yard (1 m) of solid fabric (for lining)

19¾" (50 cm) -long and ¾" (2 cm) -wide bias tape

Seam allowance: ⅜" (1 cm) for each seam.

Cutting Tips

★ Cut the fabric as shown in the illustration.
★ Determine the strap length based on the wearer's figure and height.

SEWING INSTRUCTIONS

1 Join the two strap pieces: With right sides together, sew along the seamline. Join the lining pieces in the same manner. Pin inside the seamline of the main fabric and lining fabric with the wrong sides together.

2 With the wrong sides together, face the front panel of the main fabric and lining to each other. Repeat for the back panel. Fold the seam allowance of the top edge to the inside and press. Wrap the seam allowances with bias tape and sew.

3 Fold the bag strap in half lengthwise and attach to the bag. With right sides together, sew the strap and front panel along the seamline. While sewing, double-fold the seam allowance of the base of the strap. Open the front panel slightly and make a small snip at the strap's seam allowance. Double-fold the seam allowance above the clip, pin it, and sew.

4 Repeat step 3 for the back panel. Overlock all seams.

5 Turn the bag inside out. Edgestitch the outside of the bag, connecting the stitched line to the stitches on the strap.

6 Turn the bag inside out and sew the bottom along the seamline. Overlock the seam.

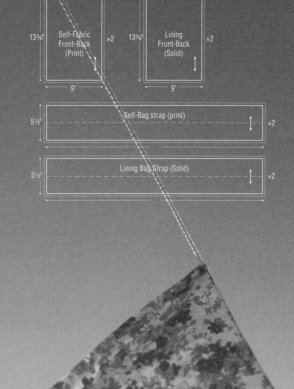

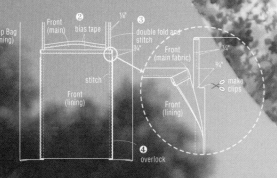

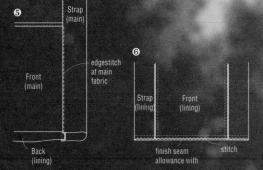

Tips: Fabric-Draping Basics

Draping fabric allows you to design and modify
clothes that are custom-fit precisely to the contours
of your body without needing patterns. Below are
instructions for modifying an existing pair of pants.
Begin by selecting the length and the width of the
legs by trying them on and pinning fabric in place.

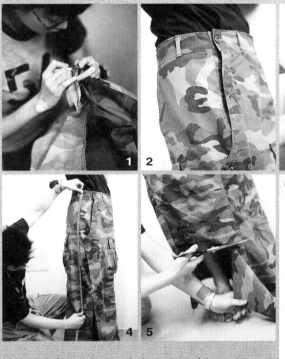

1 With a seam ripper or scissors, rip open the inner seam of the pants.
If the waist of the pants is too large, open the center back seam at the
waistband.

2 Try on the pants with the button fastened. If the back seam is open, pin it
closed to fit the desired waist size. Overlap the two front pieces and pin them
together. (The original seams that have been ripped open have folded seam
allowances. Keeping these seams folded makes shaping the garment easier.)

3 Pin the back seam. The curved hip silhouette can be created without
sewing darts. Turn down the waist slightly and pin it.

4 Determine the skirt length. If you want to design the skirt with an even
hem, mark the length with pins after measuring with a tape measure.
When cutting it, be sure to leave a 1½" (4 cm) seam allowance at the hem.

5 If you cut the skirt while you are wearing it, a natural line will be created.
When making a skirt with an uneven hem, it is better to leave ⅜" (1 cm)
seam allowance, and sew after folding once.

6 The finished look. The hem is sewn along the pinned line. Remember
to sew the previously stitched lines from the outside, because one side of
the seam will be used as is. Finish by zigzag stitching ⅜" (1 cm) along the
seam inside and trim off the excess fabric.

Designer Profile: Minimili

A fashion design team, Minimili has a trademark style that can be defined as minimal and military: thus, their name. Ji-won Song oversees brand marketing; she was a marketing manager at the Model Center, and a graduate student in fashion marketing at Yonsei University. Da-eun Jung oversees production, and is professional fashion model. Sang-wal Kim is a stylist who graduated from Tokyo Mode School. They are members of the Minimili project while maintaining their individual careers.

free-style handmade
bags & skirts

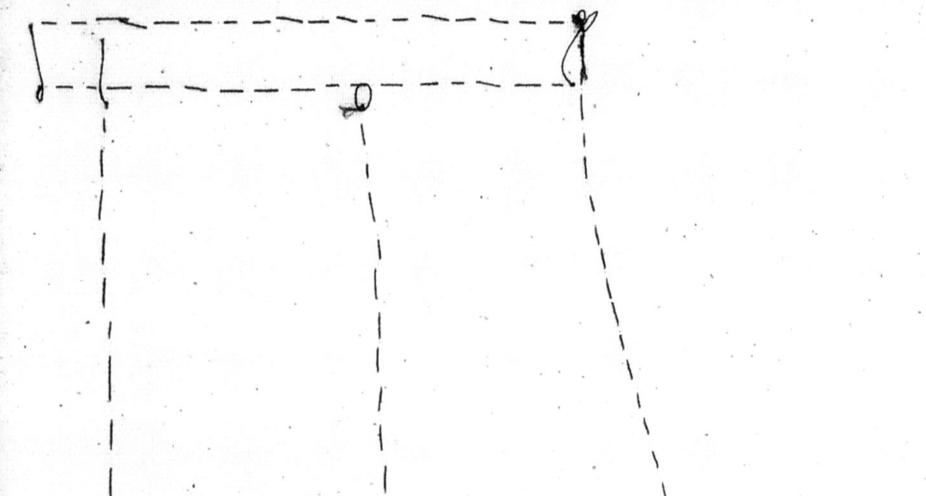